MznLnx

Missing Links Exam Preps

Exam Prep for

Marketing Research

Aaker, Kumar & Day, 9th Edition

The MznLnx Exam Prep is your link from the texbook and lecture to your exams.
The MznLnx Exam Preps are unauthorized and comprehensive reviews of your textbooks.

All material provided by MznLnx and Rico Publications (c) 2010
Textbook publishers and textbook authors do not particpate in or contribute to these reviews.

MznLnx

Rico Publications

Exam Prep for Marketing Research
9th Edition
Aaker, Kumar & Day

Publisher: Raymond Houge
Assistant Editor: Michael Rouger
Text and Cover Designer: Lisa Buckner
Marketing Manager: Sara Swagger
Project Manager, Editorial Production: Jerry Emerson
Art Director: Vernon Lowerui

Product Manager: Dave Mason
Editorial Assitant: Rachel Guzmanji
Pedagogy: Debra Long
Cover Image: Jim Reed/Getty Images
Text and Cover Printer: City Printing, Inc.
Compositor: Media Mix, Inc.

(c) 2010 Rico Publications
ALL RIGHTS RESERVED. No part of this work covered by the copyright may be reproduced or used in any form or by an means--graphic, electronic, or mechanical, including photocopying, recording, taping, Web distribution, information storage, and retrieval systems, or in any other manner--without the written permission of the publisher.

For more information about our products, contact us at:
Dave.Mason@RicoPublications.com

For permission to use material from this text or product, submit a request online to:
Dave.Mason@RicoPublications.com

Printed in the United States
ISBN:

Contents

CHAPTER 1
A Decision-Making Perspective on Marketing Intelligence — 1

CHAPTER 2
Marketing Research in Practice — 7

CHAPTER 3
The Marketing Research Process — 10

CHAPTER 4
Research Design and Implementation — 12

CHAPTER 5
Secondary Sources of Marketing Data — 20

CHAPTER 6
Standardized Sources of Marketing Data — 27

CHAPTER 7
Marketing Research on the Internet — 33

CHAPTER 8
Information Collection — 39

CHAPTER 9
Information from Respondents: Issues in Data Collection — 43

CHAPTER 10
Information from Respondents: Survey Methods — 47

CHAPTER 11
Attitude Measurement — 50

CHAPTER 12
Designing the Questionnaire — 54

CHAPTER 13
Experimentation — 55

CHAPTER 14
Sampling Fundamentals — 63

CHAPTER 15
Sample Size and Statistical Theory — 68

CHAPTER 16
Fundamentals of Data Analysis — 72

CHAPTER 17
Hypothesis Testing: Basic Concepts and Tests of Associations — 81

CHAPTER 18
Hypothesis Testing: Means and Proportions — 85

CHAPTER 19
Correlation Analysis and Regression Analysis — 89

CHAPTER 20
Discriminant and Canonical Analysis — 93

Contents (Cont.)

CHAPTER 21
   Factor and Cluster Analysis   95
CHAPTER 22
   Multidimensional Scaling and Conjoint Analysis   97
CHAPTER 23
   Presenting the Results   100
CHAPTER 24
   Traditional Applications: Product, Price, Distribution, and Promotion   101
CHAPTER 25
   Contemporary Applications   109
CHAPTER 26
   Emerging Applications   116
ANSWER KEY   128

TO THE STUDENT

COMPREHENSIVE

The *MznLnx* Exam Prep series is designed to help you pass your exams. Editors at MznLnx review your textbooks and then prepare these practice exams to help you master the textbook material. Unlike study guides, workbooks, and practice tests provided by the texbook publisher and textbook authors, *MznLnx* gives you **all** of the material in each chapter in exam form, not just samples, so you can be sure to nail your exam.

MECHANICAL

The MznLnx Exam Prep series creates exams that will help you learn the subject matter as well as test you on your understanding. Each question is designed to help you master the concept. Just working through the exams, you gain an understanding of the subject--its a simple mechanical process that produces success.

INTEGRATED STUDY GUIDE AND REVIEW

MznLnx is not just a set of exams designed to test you, its also a comprehensive review of the subject content. Each exam question is also a review of the concept, making sure that you will get the answer correct without having to go to other sources of material. You learn as you go! Its the easiest way to pass an exam.

HUMOR

Studying can be tedious and dry. MznLnx's instructional design includes moderate humor within the exam questions on occassion, to break the tedium and revitalize the brain

Chapter 1. A Decision-Making Perspective on Marketing Intelligence

1. _____ is defined by the American _____ Association as the activity, set of institutions, and processes for creating, communicating, delivering, and exchanging offerings that have value for customers, clients, partners, and society at large. The term developed from the original meaning which referred literally to going to market, as in shopping, or going to a market to sell goods or services.

_____ practice tends to be seen as a creative industry, which includes advertising, distribution and selling.

- a. Product naming
- b. Customer acquisition management
- c. Marketing
- d. Marketing myopia

2. _____ , according to Cornish, 'the process of acquiring and analyzing information in order to understand the market (both existing and potential customers); to determine the current and future needs and preferences, attitudes and behavior of the market; and to assess changes in the business environment that may affect the size and nature of the market in the future.' ('Product', 1997, p147.)

This figure shows how the interaction between variables from producers, communication channels, and consumers vary the effectiveness of _____ which affects the performance of the sales of a new product. The product is central in a circle because it helps to direct what information is gathered and how.

- a. Market intelligence
- b. Co-branding
- c. Brand parity
- d. Line extension

3. A _____ or subscription radio is a digital radio signal that is broadcast by a communications satellite, which covers a much wider geographical range than terrestrial radio signals.

For now, _____ offers a meaningful alternative to ground-based radio services in some countries, notably the United States. Mobile services, such as Sirius, XM, and Worldspace, allow listeners to roam across an entire continent, listening to the same audio programming anywhere they go.

- a. 6-3-5 Brainwriting
- b. Power III
- c. 180SearchAssistant
- d. Satellite Radio

4. _____ is the process of comparing the cost, cycle time, productivity, or quality of a specific process or method to another that is widely considered to be an industry standard or best practice. The result is often a business case for making changes in order to make improvements. The term _____ was first used by cobblers to measure ones feet for shoes.
- a. Business strategy
- b. Strategic group
- c. Switching cost
- d. Benchmarking

5. _____ is a technique employed by forensic scientists to assist in the identification of individuals on the basis of their respective DNA profiles.

Although 99.9% of human DNA sequences are the same in every person, enough of the DNA is different to distinguish one individual from another. _____ uses repetitive sequences that vary a lot, called variable number tandem repeats

a. F-statistics
b. DNA profiling
c. 180SearchAssistant
d. Power III

6. Consumer market research is a form of applied sociology that concentrates on understanding the behaviours, whims and preferences, of consumers in a market-based economy, and aims to understand the effects and comparative success of marketing campaigns. The field of consumer _____ as a statistical science was pioneered by Arthur Nielsen with the founding of the ACNielsen Company in 1923.

Thus _____ is the systematic and objective identification, collection, analysis, and dissemination of information for the purpose of assisting management in decision making related to the identification and solution of problems and opportunities in marketing.

a. Logit analysis
b. Marketing research process
c. Marketing research
d. Focus group

7. Procter is a surname, and may also refer to:

- Bryan Waller Procter (pseud. Barry Cornwall), English poet
- Goodwin Procter, American law firm
- _____, consumer products multinational

a. Flyer
b. Black PRies
c. Convergent
d. Procter ' Gamble

8. _____ is an advertisement in which a particular product specifically mentions a competitor by name for the express purpose of showing why the competitor is inferior to the product naming it.

This should not be confused with parody advertisements, where a fictional product is being advertised for the purpose of poking fun at the particular advertisement, nor should it be confused with the use of a coined brand name for the purpose of comparing the product without actually naming an actual competitor. ('Wikipedia tastes better and is less filling than the Encyclopedia Galactica.')

In the 1980s, during what has been referred to as the cola wars, soft-drink manufacturer Pepsi ran a series of advertisements where people, caught on hidden camera, in a blind taste test, chose Pepsi over rival Coca-Cola.

a. GL-70
b. Cost per conversion
c. Heavy-up
d. Comparative advertising

9. A _____ is an entity that provides services to other entities. Usually this refers to a business that provides subscription or web service to other businesses or individuals. Examples of these services include Internet access, Mobile phone operator, and web application hosting.

a. Cross-selling
b. Freebie marketing
c. Yield management
d. Service provider

10. _____ can be regarded as an outcome of mental processes (cognitive process) leading to the selection of a course of action among several alternatives. Every _____ process produces a final choice. The output can be an action or an opinion of choice.
   a. Decision making
   b. 180SearchAssistant
   c. 6-3-5 Brainwriting
   d. Power III

11. A _____ is a form of qualitative research in which a group of people are asked about their attitude towards a product, service, concept, advertisement, idea, or packaging. Questions are asked in an interactive group setting where participants are free to talk with other group members.

Ernest Dichter originated the idea of having a 'group therapy' for products and this process is what became known as a _____.

   a. Cross tabulation
   b. Logit analysis
   c. Marketing research process
   d. Focus group

12. A _____ is a plan of action designed to achieve a particular goal.

_____ is different from tactics. In military terms, tactics is concerned with the conduct of an engagement while _____ is concerned with how different engagements are linked.

   a. Strategy
   b. Power III
   c. 6-3-5 Brainwriting
   d. 180SearchAssistant

13. A supply chain is the system of organizations, people, technology, activities, information and resources involved in moving a product or service from _____ to customer. Supply chain activities transform natural resources, raw materials and components into a finished product that is delivered to the end customer. In sophisticated supply chain systems, used products may re-enter the supply chain at any point where residual value is recyclable.
   a. Bringin' Home the Oil
   b. Rebate
   c. Product line extension
   d. Supplier

14. _____ is a term that refers both to:

   - a formal discipline used to help appraise, or assess, the case for a project or proposal, which itself is a process known as project appraisal; and
   - an informal approach to making decisions of any kind.

Under both definitions the process involves, whether explicitly or implicitly, weighing the total expected costs against the total expected benefits of one or more actions in order to choose the best or most profitable option. The formal process is often referred to as either CBA (_____) or BCost-benefit analysis

A hallmark of CBA is that all benefits and all costs are expressed in money terms, and are adjusted for the time value of money, so that all flows of benefits and flows of project costs over time (which tend to occur at different points in time) are expressed on a common basis in terms of their 'present value.' Closely related, but slightly different, formal techniques include Cost-effectiveness analysis, Economic impact analysis, Fiscal impact analysis and Social Return on Investment(SROI) analysis. The latter builds upon the logic of _____, but differs in that it is explicitly designed to inform the practical decision-making of enterprise managers and investors focused on optimising their social and environmental impacts.

a. 180SearchAssistant
b. 6-3-5 Brainwriting
c. Power III
d. Cost-benefit analysis

15. _____ is a branch of philosophy which seeks to address questions about morality, such as how a moral outcome can be achieved in a specific situation (applied _____), how moral values should be determined (normative _____), what moral values people actually abide by (descriptive _____), what the fundamental semantic, ontological, and epistemic nature of _____ or morality is (meta-_____), and how moral capacity or moral agency develops and what its nature is (moral psychology.)

Socrates was one of the first Greek philosophers to encourage both scholars and the common citizen to turn their attention from the outside world to the condition of man. In this view, Knowledge having a bearing on human life was placed highest, all other knowledge being secondary.

a. AMAX
b. ACNielsen
c. ADTECH
d. Ethics

16. _____ is the practice of individuals including commercial businesses, governments and institutions, facilitating the sale of their products or services to other companies or organizations that in turn resell them, use them as components in products or services they offer _____ is also called business-to-_____ for short. (Note that while marketing to government entities shares some of the same dynamics of organizational marketing, B2G Marketing is meaningfully different.)

a. Law of disruption
b. Disruptive technology
c. Mass marketing
d. Business marketing

17. _____ a research method involving the use of questionnaires and/or statistical surveys to gather data about people and their thoughts and behaviours.

a. T-test
b. Z-test
c. Control chart
d. Survey Research

18. _____, known also as _____entification (Caller IDD) is a telephone service, available on POTS (Plain Old Telephone Service) lines, that transmits a caller's number to the called party's telephone equipment during the ringing signal _____ can also provide a name associated with the calling telephone number, for a higher fee. The information made available to the called party may be made visible on a telephone's own display or on a separate attached device.

a. 180SearchAssistant
b. 6-3-5 Brainwriting
c. Power III
d. Caller ID

19. _____ refer to a collection of facts usually collected as the result of experience, observation or experiment or a set of premises. This may consist of numbers, words particularly as measurements or observations of a set of variables. _____ are often viewed as a lowest level of abstraction from which information and knowledge are derived.
   a. Data
   b. Sample size
   c. Pearson product-moment correlation coefficient
   d. Mean

20. Electronic tagging is a form of non-surreptitious surveillance consisting of an electronic device attached to a person or vehicle, especially certain criminals, allowing their whereabouts to be monitored. In general, devices locate themselves using GPS and report their position back to a control centre, e.g. via the Cellular phone network. This form of criminal sentencing is known under different names in different countries, for example in New Zealand it is referred to as 'home detention', and in North America '_____' is a more common term.
   a. AMAX
   b. ADTECH
   c. ACNielsen
   d. Electronic monitoring

21. An _____ is a survey of public opinion from a particular sample. _____s are usually designed to represent the opinions of a population by conducting a series of questions and then extrapolating generalities in ratio or within confidence intervals.

The first known example of an _____ was a local straw poll conducted by The Harrisburg Pennsylvanian in 1824, showing Andrew Jackson leading John Quincy Adams by 335 votes to 169 in the contest for the United States Presidency.

   a. ADTECH
   b. AMAX
   c. ACNielsen
   d. Opinion poll

22. _____ is the ability of an individual or group to seclude themselves or information about themselves and thereby reveal themselves selectively. The boundaries and content of what is considered private differ among cultures and individuals, but share basic common themes. _____ is sometimes related to anonymity, the wish to remain unnoticed or unidentified in the public realm.
   a. 6-3-5 Brainwriting
   b. Power III
   c. 180SearchAssistant
   d. Privacy

23. A _____, in the field of business and marketing, is a geographic region or demographic group used to gauge the viability of a product or service in the mass market prior to a wide scale roll-out. The criteria used to judge the acceptability of a _____ region or group include:

   1. a population that is demographically similar to the proposed target market; and
   2. relative isolation from densely populated media markets so that advertising to the test audience can be efficient and economical.

The _____ ideally aims to duplicate 'everything' - promotion and distribution as well as `product' - on a smaller scale. The technique replicates, typically in one area, what is planned to occur in a national launch; and the results are very carefully monitored, so that they can be extrapolated to projected national results. The `area' may be any one of the following:

- Television area
- Test town
- Residential neighborhood
- Test site

A number of decisions have to be taken about any _____:

- Which _____?
- What is to be tested?
- How long a test?
- What are the success criteria?

The simple go or no-go decision, together with the related reduction of risk, is normally the main justification for the expense of _____s. At the same time, however, such _____s can be used to test specific elements of a new product's marketing mix; possibly the version of the product itself, the promotional message and media spend, the distribution channels and the price.

a. Power III
c. 180SearchAssistant
b. Test market
d. Preadolescence

24. _____ has been defined by the International Organization for Standardization (ISO) as 'ensuring that information is accessible only to those authorized to have access' and is one of the cornerstones of information security. _____ is one of the design goals for many cryptosystems, made possible in practice by the techniques of modern cryptography.

_____ also refers to an ethical principle associated with several professions (e.g., medicine, law, religion, professional psychology, and journalism.)

a. 6-3-5 Brainwriting
c. 180SearchAssistant
b. Confidentiality
d. Power III

Chapter 2. Marketing Research in Practice

1. A _____ is a structured collection of records or data that is stored in a computer system. The structure is achieved by organizing the data according to a _____ model. The model in most common use today is the relational model.
   a. Power III
   b. 6-3-5 Brainwriting
   c. 180SearchAssistant
   d. Database

2. _____ is a form of direct marketing using databases of customers or potential customers to generate personalized communications in order to promote a product or service for marketing purposes. The method of communication can be any addressable medium, as in direct marketing.

   The distinction between direct and _____ stems primarily from the attention paid to the analysis of data.

   a. Power III
   b. Direct Marketing Associations
   c. Direct marketing
   d. Database marketing

3. _____ constitute a class of computer-based information systems including knowledge-based systems that support decision-making activities.

   _____ are a specific class of computerized information system that supports business and organizational decision-making activities. A properly-designed _____ is an interactive software-based system intended to help decision makers compile useful information from raw data, documents, personal knowledge, and/or business models to identify and solve problems and make decisions.

   a. 180SearchAssistant
   b. 6-3-5 Brainwriting
   c. Power III
   d. Decision support systems

4. A supply chain is the system of organizations, people, technology, activities, information and resources involved in moving a product or service from _____ to customer. Supply chain activities transform natural resources, raw materials and components into a finished product that is delivered to the end customer. In sophisticated supply chain systems, used products may re-enter the supply chain at any point where residual value is recyclable.
   a. Supplier
   b. Product line extension
   c. Bringin' Home the Oil
   d. Rebate

5. _____ is defined by the American _____ Association as the activity, set of institutions, and processes for creating, communicating, delivering, and exchanging offerings that have value for customers, clients, partners, and society at large. The term developed from the original meaning which referred literally to going to market, as in shopping, or going to a market to sell goods or services.

   _____ practice tends to be seen as a creative industry, which includes advertising, distribution and selling.

   a. Marketing
   b. Product naming
   c. Customer acquisition management
   d. Marketing myopia

6. _____ is an information system that helps with decision-making in the formation of a marketing plan. The reason for using an MKDSS is because it helps to support the software vendors' planning strategy for marketing products; it can help to identify advantageous levels of pricing, advertising spending, and advertising copy for the firm's products (Arinze, 1990.) This helps determines the firms marketing mix for product software.

a. Power III
b. 6-3-5 Brainwriting
c. Marketing decision support systems
d. 180SearchAssistant

7. In probability theory and statistics, the _____ of a random variable, probability distribution, or sample is a measure of statistical dispersion, averaging the squared distance of its possible values from the expected value (mean.) Whereas the mean is a way to describe the location of a distribution, the _____ is a way to capture its scale or degree of being spread out. The unit of _____ is the square of the unit of the original variable.
   a. Standard deviation
   b. Sample size
   c. Variance
   d. Correlation

8. Consumer market research is a form of applied sociology that concentrates on understanding the behaviours, whims and preferences, of consumers in a market-based economy, and aims to understand the effects and comparative success of marketing campaigns. The field of consumer _____ as a statistical science was pioneered by Arthur Nielsen with the founding of the ACNielsen Company in 1923.

Thus _____ is the systematic and objective identification, collection, analysis, and dissemination of information for the purpose of assisting management in decision making related to the identification and solution of problems and opportunities in marketing.

   a. Marketing research
   b. Marketing research process
   c. Logit analysis
   d. Focus group

9. An _____ is the manufacturing of a good or service within a category. Although _____ is a broad term for any kind of economic production, in economics and urban planning _____ is a synonym for the secondary sector, which is a type of economic activity involved in the manufacturing of raw materials into goods and products.

There are four key industrial economic sectors: the primary sector, largely raw material extraction industries such as mining and farming; the secondary sector, involving refining, construction, and manufacturing; the tertiary sector, which deals with services (such as law and medicine) and distribution of manufactured goods; and the quaternary sector, a relatively new type of knowledge _____ focusing on technological research, design and development such as computer programming, and biochemistry.

   a. ACNielsen
   b. ADTECH
   c. AMAX
   d. Industry

10. _____ is the practice of individuals including commercial businesses, governments and institutions, facilitating the sale of their products or services to other companies or organizations that in turn resell them, use them as components in products or services they offer _____ is also called business-to-_____ for short. (Note that while marketing to government entities shares some of the same dynamics of organizational marketing, B2G Marketing is meaningfully different.)
   a. Law of disruption
   b. Business marketing
   c. Mass marketing
   d. Disruptive technology

11. _____ a research method involving the use of questionnaires and/or statistical surveys to gather data about people and their thoughts and behaviours.

a. Z-test
c. T-test
b. Survey Research
d. Control chart

12. In economics, an externality or spillover of an economic transaction is an impact on a party that is not directly involved in the transaction. In such a case, prices do not reflect the full costs or benefits in production or consumption of a product or service. A positive impact is called an _____ benefit, while a negative impact is called an _____ cost.
   a. ACNielsen
   b. ADTECH
   c. AMAX
   d. External

13. _____ is an advertisement in which a particular product specifically mentions a competitor by name for the express purpose of showing why the competitor is inferior to the product naming it.

This should not be confused with parody advertisements, where a fictional product is being advertised for the purpose of poking fun at the particular advertisement, nor should it be confused with the use of a coined brand name for the purpose of comparing the product without actually naming an actual competitor. ('Wikipedia tastes better and is less filling than the Encyclopedia Galactica.')

In the 1980s, during what has been referred to as the cola wars, soft-drink manufacturer Pepsi ran a series of advertisements where people, caught on hidden camera, in a blind taste test, chose Pepsi over rival Coca-Cola.

   a. Cost per conversion
   b. Comparative advertising
   c. Heavy-up
   d. GL-70

14. _____ is the assignment of objects into groups (called clusters) so that objects from the same cluster are more similar to each other than objects from different clusters. Often similarity is assessed according to a distance measure. _____ is a common technique for statistical data analysis, which is used in many fields, including machine learning, data mining, pattern recognition, image analysis and bioinformatics.
   a. Clustering
   b. Just-In-Case
   c. Comparison-Shopping agent
   d. Developed country

15. Human beings are also considered to be _____ because they have the ability to change raw materials into valuable _____. The term Human _____ can also be defined as the skills, energies, talents, abilities and knowledge that are used for the production of goods or the rendering of services. While taking into account human beings as _____, the following things have to be kept in mind:

- The size of the population
- The capabilities of the individuals in that population

Many _____ cannot be consumed in their original form. They have to be processed in order to change them into more usable commodities.

   a. Resources
   b. 6-3-5 Brainwriting
   c. Power III
   d. 180SearchAssistant

Chapter 3. The Marketing Research Process

1. _____ is defined by the American _____ Association as the activity, set of institutions, and processes for creating, communicating, delivering, and exchanging offerings that have value for customers, clients, partners, and society at large. The term developed from the original meaning which referred literally to going to market, as in shopping, or going to a market to sell goods or services.

_____ practice tends to be seen as a creative industry, which includes advertising, distribution and selling.

   a. Product naming
   c. Customer acquisition management
   b. Marketing myopia
   d. Marketing

2. Consumer market research is a form of applied sociology that concentrates on understanding the behaviours, whims and preferences, of consumers in a market-based economy, and aims to understand the effects and comparative success of marketing campaigns. The field of consumer _____ as a statistical science was pioneered by Arthur Nielsen with the founding of the ACNielsen Company in 1923.

Thus _____ is the systematic and objective identification, collection, analysis, and dissemination of information for the purpose of assisting management in decision making related to the identification and solution of problems and opportunities in marketing.

   a. Marketing research
   c. Logit analysis
   b. Marketing research process
   d. Focus group

3. A personal and cultural _____ is a relative ethic _____, an assumption upon which implementation can be extrapolated. A _____ system is a set of consistent _____s and measures that is soo not true. A principle _____ is a foundation upon which other _____s and measures of integrity are based.
   a. Value
   c. Perceptual maps
   b. Package-on-Package
   d. Supreme Court of the United States

4. _____ is the practice of individuals including commercial businesses, governments and institutions, facilitating the sale of their products or services to other companies or organizations that in turn resell them, use them as components in products or services they offer _____ is also called business-to-_____ for short. (Note that while marketing to government entities shares some of the same dynamics of organizational marketing, B2G Marketing is meaningfully different.)
   a. Disruptive technology
   c. Mass marketing
   b. Law of disruption
   d. Business marketing

5. A supply chain is the system of organizations, people, technology, activities, information and resources involved in moving a product or service from _____ to customer. Supply chain activities transform natural resources, raw materials and components into a finished product that is delivered to the end customer. In sophisticated supply chain systems, used products may re-enter the supply chain at any point where residual value is recyclable.
   a. Supplier
   c. Product line extension
   b. Rebate
   d. Bringin' Home the Oil

6. A _____ applies the scientific method to experimentally examine an intervention in the real world (or as many experimental economists like to say, naturally-occurring environments) rather than in the laboratory. _____s, like lab experiments, generally randomize subjects (or other sampling units) into treatment and control groups and compare outcomes between these groups. Clinical trials of pharmaceuticals are one example of _____s.

a. 180SearchAssistant
b. Response variable
c. Power III
d. Field experiment

7. _____ is statistical inference in which evidence or observations are used to update or to newly infer the probability that a hypothesis may be true. The name 'Bayesian' comes from the frequent use of Bayes' theorem in the inference process. Bayes' theorem was derived from the work of the Reverend Thomas Bayes.
   a. Chi-square test
   b. Heteroskedastic
   c. Standard deviation
   d. Bayesian inference

Chapter 4. Research Design and Implementation

1. A number of different _____s are indicated below.

    - Randomized controlled trial
        - Double-blind randomized trial
        - Single-blind randomized trial
        - Non-blind trial
    - Nonrandomized trial (quasi-experiment)
        - Interrupted time series design (measures on a sample or a series of samples from the same population are obtained several times before and after a manipulated event or a naturally occurring event) - considered a type of quasi-experiment

    - Cohort study
        - Prospective cohort
        - Retrospective cohort
        - Time series study
    - Case-control study
        - Nested case-control study
    - Cross-sectional study
        - Community survey (a type of cross-sectional study)

    When choosing a _____, many factors must be taken into account. Different types of studies are subject to different types of bias. For example, recall bias is likely to occur in cross-sectional or case-control studies where subjects are asked to recall exposure to risk factors.

    a. Power III
    c. Study design
    b. 180SearchAssistant
    d. Longitudinal studies

2. _____ is a type of research conducted because a problem has not been clearly defined. _____ helps determine the best research design, data collection method and selection of subjects. Given its fundamental nature, _____ often concludes that a perceived problem does not actually exist.
    a. IDDEA
    c. Exploratory research
    b. Intent scale translation
    d. ACNielsen

3. _____ describes data and characteristics about the population or phenomenon being studied. _____ answers the questions who, what, where, when and how.

    Although the data description is factual, accurate and systematic, the research cannot describe what caused a situation.

    a. Descriptive research
    c. Power III
    b. Sampling error
    d. Two-tailed test

4. _____ is defined by the American _____ Association as the activity, set of institutions, and processes for creating, communicating, delivering, and exchanging offerings that have value for customers, clients, partners, and society at large. The term developed from the original meaning which referred literally to going to market, as in shopping, or going to a market to sell goods or services.

Chapter 4. Research Design and Implementation 13

_____ practice tends to be seen as a creative industry, which includes advertising, distribution and selling.

a. Product naming
c. Customer acquisition management
b. Marketing myopia
d. Marketing

5. _____ are an emerging and developing area in market research making use of developments in Web 2.0 technologies and online communities. They allow qualitative research to be conducted efficiently and deeply online.

Both public and private online communities offer opportunities for research, but many brands are wary of sharing company information openly.

a. ACNielsen
c. AMAX
b. Online research communities
d. ADTECH

6. A _____, in the field of business and marketing, is a geographic region or demographic group used to gauge the viability of a product or service in the mass market prior to a wide scale roll-out. The criteria used to judge the acceptability of a _____ region or group include:

1. a population that is demographically similar to the proposed target market; and
2. relative isolation from densely populated media markets so that advertising to the test audience can be efficient and economical.

The _____ ideally aims to duplicate 'everything' - promotion and distribution as well as `product' - on a smaller scale. The technique replicates, typically in one area, what is planned to occur in a national launch; and the results are very carefully monitored, so that they can be extrapolated to projected national results. The `area' may be any one of the following:

- Television area
- Test town
- Residential neighborhood
- Test site

A number of decisions have to be taken about any _____:

- Which _____?
- What is to be tested?
- How long a test?
- What are the success criteria?

The simple go or no-go decision, together with the related reduction of risk, is normally the main justification for the expense of _____s. At the same time, however, such _____s can be used to test specific elements of a new product's marketing mix; possibly the version of the product itself, the promotional message and media spend, the distribution channels and the price.

Chapter 4. Research Design and Implementation

a. Power III
b. Preadolescence
c. 180SearchAssistant
d. Test market

7. Procter is a surname, and may also refer to:

   - Bryan Waller Procter (pseud. Barry Cornwall), English poet
   - Goodwin Procter, American law firm
   - _____, consumer products multinational

a. Convergent
b. Procter ' Gamble
c. Black PRies
d. Flyer

8. _____ in economics and business is the result of an exchange and from that trade we assign a numerical monetary value to a good, service or asset. If I trade 4 apples for an orange, the _____ of an orange is 4 - apples. Inversely, the _____ of an apple is 1/4 oranges.

a. Contribution margin-based pricing
b. Discounts and allowances
c. Pricing
d. Price

9. A _____ is a plan of action designed to achieve a particular goal.

_____ is different from tactics. In military terms, tactics is concerned with the conduct of an engagement while _____ is concerned with how different engagements are linked.

a. 180SearchAssistant
b. 6-3-5 Brainwriting
c. Power III
d. Strategy

10. _____ is a term for unprocessed data, it is also known as primary data. It is a relative term _____ can be input to a computer program or used in manual analysis procedures such as gathering statistics from a survey.

a. Chief marketing officer
b. Shoppers Food ' Pharmacy
c. Product manager
d. Raw data

11. Combining Existing _____ Sources with New Primary Data Sources

Imagine that we could get hold of a good collection of surveys taken in earlier years, such as detailed studies about changes going on in this phase and hopefully additional studies in the years to come. Analyzing this data base over time could give us a good picture of what changes actually have taken place in the orientation of the population and of the extent to which new technical concepts did have an impact on subgroups of the population. Furthermore, data archives can help to prepare studies on change over time by monitoring what questions have been asked in earlier years and alerting principal investigators to important questions which should be repeated in planned research projects.

a. 180SearchAssistant
b. 6-3-5 Brainwriting
c. Power III
d. Secondary data

Chapter 4. Research Design and Implementation

12. _____ refer to a collection of facts usually collected as the result of experience, observation or experiment or a set of premises. This may consist of numbers, words particularly as measurements or observations of a set of variables. _____ are often viewed as a lowest level of abstraction from which information and knowledge are derived.
   a. Data
   b. Pearson product-moment correlation coefficient
   c. Mean
   d. Sample size

13. _____ is a term used to describe a process of preparing and collecting data - for example as part of a process improvement or similar project.

_____ usually takes place early on in an improvement project, and is often formalised through a _____ Plan which often contains the following activity.

   1. Pre collection activity - Agree goals, target data, definitions, methods
   2. Collection - _____
   3. Present Findings - usually involves some form of sorting analysis and/or presentation.

A formal _____ process is necessary as it ensures that data gathered is both defined and accurate and that subsequent decisions based on arguments embodied in the findings are valid . The process provides both a baseline from which to measure from and in certain cases a target on what to improve. Types of _____ 1-By mail questionnaires 2-By personal interview

- Six sigma
- Sampling (statistics)

   a. 180SearchAssistant
   b. 6-3-5 Brainwriting
   c. Power III
   d. Data collection

14. A _____ is a research instrument consisting of a series of questions and other prompts for the purpose of gathering information from respondents. Although they are often designed for statistical analysis of the responses, this is not always the case. The _____ was invented by Sir Francis Galton.
   a. Mystery shopping
   b. Market research
   c. Mystery shoppers
   d. Questionnaire

15. _____ is that part of statistical practice concerned with the selection of individual observations intended to yield some knowledge about a population of concern, especially for the purposes of statistical inference. Each observation measures one or more properties (weight, location, etc.) of an observable entity enumerated to distinguish objects or individuals.
   a. Richard Buckminster 'Bucky' Fuller
   b. AStore
   c. Sports Marketing Group
   d. Sampling

16. _____ is the realization of an application idea, model, design, specification, standard, algorithm an _____ is a realization of a technical specification or algorithm as a program, software component, or other computer system. Many _____s may exist for a given specification or standard.

Chapter 4. Research Design and Implementation

a. ACNielsen
b. AMAX
c. Implementation
d. ADTECH

17. A personal and cultural _____ is a relative ethic _____, an assumption upon which implementation can be extrapolated. A _____ system is a set of consistent _____s and measures that is soo not true. A principle _____ is a foundation upon which other _____s and measures of integrity are based.
   a. Package-on-Package
   b. Supreme Court of the United States
   c. Perceptual maps
   d. Value

18.

_____ is a systematic method to improve the 'value' of goods or products and services by using an examination of function. Value, as defined, is the ratio of function to cost. Value can therefore be increased by either improving the function or reducing the cost.

   a. Power III
   b. Productivity
   c. 180SearchAssistant
   d. Value engineering

19. In economics, business, retail, and accounting, a _____ is the value of money that has been used up to produce something, and hence is not available for use anymore. In economics, a _____ is an alternative that is given up as a result of a decision. In business, the _____ may be one of acquisition, in which case the amount of money expended to acquire it is counted as _____.
   a. Cost
   b. Transaction cost
   c. Variable cost
   d. Fixed costs

20. _____ generally refers to a list of all planned expenses and revenues. It is a plan for saving and spending. A _____ is an important concept in microeconomics, which uses a _____ line to illustrate the trade-offs between two or more goods.
   a. Power III
   b. 6-3-5 Brainwriting
   c. 180SearchAssistant
   d. Budget

21. The _____, abbreviated _____ is a mathematically based algorithm for scheduling a set of project activities. It is an important tool for effective project management.

It was developed in the 1950s by the US Navy when trying to better organize the building of submarines and later, especially, when building nuclear submarines.

   a. Power III
   b. Critical path method
   c. 6-3-5 Brainwriting
   d. 180SearchAssistant

22. A _____ is a type of bar chart that illustrates a project schedule. A _____ illustrates the start and finish dates of the terminal elements and summary elements of a project. Terminal elements and summary elements comprise the work breakdown structure of the project.
   a. GANTT chart
   b. 180SearchAssistant
   c. 6-3-5 Brainwriting
   d. Power III

Chapter 4. Research Design and Implementation

23. The _____, is a model for project management designed to analyze and represent the tasks involved in completing a given project.

_____ is a method to analyze the involved tasks in completing a given project, especially the time needed to complete each task, and identifying the minimum time needed to complete the total project.

PERT was developed primarily to simplify the planning and scheduling of large and complex projects.

a. 180SearchAssistant
c. Power III

b. Program evaluation and review technique
d. 6-3-5 Brainwriting

24. _____ is systematic determination of merit, worth, and significance of something or someone using criteria against a set of standards. _____ often is used to characterize and appraise subjects of interest in a wide range of human enterprises, including the arts, criminal justice, foundations and non-profit organizations, government, health care, and other human services.

Depending on the topic of interest, there are professional groups which look to the quality and rigor of the _____ process.

a. ADTECH
c. AMAX

b. ACNielsen
d. Evaluation

25. Consumer market research is a form of applied sociology that concentrates on understanding the behaviours, whims and preferences, of consumers in a market-based economy, and aims to understand the effects and comparative success of marketing campaigns. The field of consumer _____ as a statistical science was pioneered by Arthur Nielsen with the founding of the ACNielsen Company in 1923 .

Thus _____ is the systematic and objective identification, collection, analysis, and dissemination of information for the purpose of assisting management in decision making related to the identification and solution of problems and opportunities in marketing.

a. Marketing research process
c. Logit analysis

b. Focus group
d. Marketing research

26. In statistics, _____ or estimation error is the error caused by observing a sample instead of the whole population.

An estimate of a quantity of interest, such as an average or percentage, will generally be subject to sample-to-sample variation. These variations in the possible sample values of a statistic can theoretically be expressed as _____s, although in practice the exact _____ is typically unknown.

a. Two-tailed test
c. Varimax rotation

b. Power III
d. Sampling error

Chapter 4. Research Design and Implementation

27. _____ is a process of gathering, modeling, and transforming data with the goal of highlighting useful information, suggesting conclusions, and supporting decision making. _____ has multiple facets and approaches, encompassing diverse techniques under a variety of names, in different business, science, and social science domains.

Data mining is a particular _____ technique that focuses on modeling and knowledge discovery for predictive rather than purely descriptive purposes.

a. 180SearchAssistant
b. Power III
c. Data analysis
d. 6-3-5 Brainwriting

28. A _____ is an error that occurs when a person performs an action on an object that is not the object intended. This error can be very disorienting and usually causes a brief loss of situation awareness or automation surprise if noticed right away. But much worse, if it goes unnoticed, it could cause more serious problems.

a. Description error
b. Motivation
c. 180SearchAssistant
d. Power III

29. _____ is a standard point of view or personal prejudice. especially when the tendency interferes with the ability to be impartial, unprejudiced, or objective. The term _____ed is used to describe an action, judgment, or other outcome influenced by a prejudged perspective.

a. Power III
b. Bias
c. 6-3-5 Brainwriting
d. 180SearchAssistant

30. In statistics, _____ has two related meanings:

- the arithmetic _____
- the expected value of a random variable, which is also called the population _____.

It is sometimes stated that the '_____' _____s average. This is incorrect if '_____' is taken in the specific sense of 'arithmetic _____' as there are different types of averages: the _____, median, and mode. For instance, average house prices almost always use the median value for the average. These three types of averages are all measures of locations.

a. Heteroskedastic
b. Confidence interval
c. Standard normal distribution
d. Mean

31. A _____ is an explicit set of requirements to be satisfied by a material, product, or service.

In engineering, manufacturing, and business, it is vital for suppliers, purchasers, and users of materials, products, or services to understand and agree upon all requirements. A _____ is a type of a standard which is often referenced by a contract or procurement document.

a. Specification
b. Product development
c. Product optimization
d. New product development

32. _____ is a mathematical science pertaining to the collection, analysis, interpretation or explanation, and presentation of data. It also provides tools for prediction and forecasting based on data. It is applicable to a wide variety of academic disciplines, from the natural and social sciences to the humanities, government and business.
   a. Type I error
   b. Statistics
   c. Median
   d. Null hypothesis

Chapter 5. Secondary Sources of Marketing Data

1. An _____ is the manufacturing of a good or service within a category. Although _____ is a broad term for any kind of economic production, in economics and urban planning _____ is a synonym for the secondary sector, which is a type of economic activity involved in the manufacturing of raw materials into goods and products.

There are four key industrial economic sectors: the primary sector, largely raw material extraction industries such as mining and farming; the secondary sector, involving refining, construction, and manufacturing; the tertiary sector, which deals with services (such as law and medicine) and distribution of manufactured goods; and the quaternary sector, a relatively new type of knowledge _____ focusing on technological research, design and development such as computer programming, and biochemistry.

   a. ADTECH
   b. AMAX
   c. ACNielsen
   d. Industry

2. The _____ or _____ is used by business and government to classify and measure economic activity in Canada, Mexico and the United States. It has largely replaced the older Standard Industrial Classification system; however, certain government departments and agencies, such as the U.S. Securities and Exchange Commission (SEC), still use the SIC codes.

The _____ numbering system is a six-digit code.

   a. North American Industry Classification System
   b. 180SearchAssistant
   c. Power III
   d. 6-3-5 Brainwriting

3. _____ refer to a collection of facts usually collected as the result of experience, observation or experiment or a set of premises. This may consist of numbers, words particularly as measurements or observations of a set of variables. _____ are often viewed as a lowest level of abstraction from which information and knowledge are derived.
   a. Mean
   b. Sample size
   c. Pearson product-moment correlation coefficient
   d. Data

4. Combining Existing _____ Sources with New Primary Data Sources

Imagine that we could get hold of a good collection of surveys taken in earlier years, such as detailed studies about changes going on in this phase and hopefully additional studies in the years to come. Analyzing this data base over time could give us a good picture of what changes actually have taken place in the orientation of the population and of the extent to which new technical concepts did have an impact on subgroups of the population. Furthermore, data archives can help to prepare studies on change over time by monitoring what questions have been asked in earlier years and alerting principal investigators to important questions which should be repeated in planned research projects.

   a. Power III
   b. 180SearchAssistant
   c. 6-3-5 Brainwriting
   d. Secondary data

5. _____ is a technique employed by forensic scientists to assist in the identification of individuals on the basis of their respective DNA profiles.

Chapter 5. Secondary Sources of Marketing Data 21

Although 99.9% of human DNA sequences are the same in every person, enough of the DNA is different to distinguish one individual from another. _____ uses repetitive sequences that vary a lot, called variable number tandem repeats

    a. Power III
    c. 180SearchAssistant
    b. F-statistics
    d. DNA profiling

6. _____ describes the situation when output from (or information about the result of) an event or phenomenon in the past will influence the same event/phenomenon in the present or future. When an event is part of a chain of cause-and-effect that forms a circuit or loop, then the event is said to 'feed back' into itself.

_____ is also a synonym for:

- _____ Signal; the information about the initial event that is the basis for subsequent modification of the event.
- _____ Loop; the causal path that leads from the initial generation of the _____ signal to the subsequent modification of the event.

_____ is a mechanism, process or signal that is looped back to control a system within itself. Such a loop is called a _____ loop.

    a. Power III
    c. 180SearchAssistant
    b. 6-3-5 Brainwriting
    d. Feedback

7. _____ is the process of gathering and analysing information regarding customers; their details and their activities, in order to build deeper and more effective customer relationships and improve strategic decision making.

Consumer Intelligence is also the name of a leading company within the UK Research industry that is referenced in large number of Advertising campaigns by companies such as Asda, Budget Compare The Market, Churchill, Direct Line, MoneySupermarket, Norwich Union and many others.

_____ is a key component of effective Customer Relationship Management, and when effectively implemented it is a rich source of insight into the behaviour and experience of a company's customer base.

    a. Pop-up ads
    c. Project Portfolio Management
    b. Power III
    d. Customer intelligence

8. _____, a business term, is a measure of how products and services supplied by a company meet or surpass customer expectation. It is seen as a key performance indicator within business and is part of the four perspectives of a Balanced Scorecard.

In a competitive marketplace where businesses compete for customers, _____ is seen as a key differentiator and increasingly has become a key element of business strategy.

Chapter 5. Secondary Sources of Marketing Data

a. Customer base
b. Customer satisfaction
c. Psychological pricing
d. Supplier diversity

9. A _____ is a structured collection of records or data that is stored in a computer system. The structure is achieved by organizing the data according to a _____ model. The model in most common use today is the relational model.
a. Power III
b. 180SearchAssistant
c. 6-3-5 Brainwriting
d. Database

10. In economics, an externality or spillover of an economic transaction is an impact on a party that is not directly involved in the transaction. In such a case, prices do not reflect the full costs or benefits in production or consumption of a product or service. A positive impact is called an _____ benefit, while a negative impact is called an _____ cost.
a. AMAX
b. External
c. ACNielsen
d. ADTECH

11. _____ is one of the four elements of marketing mix. An organization or set of organizations (go-betweens) involved in the process of making a product or service available for use or consumption by a consumer or business user.

The other three parts of the marketing mix are product, pricing, and promotion.

a. Japan Advertising Photographers' Association
b. Comparison-Shopping agent
c. Better Living Through Chemistry
d. Distribution

12. _____ is defined by the American _____ Association as the activity, set of institutions, and processes for creating, communicating, delivering, and exchanging offerings that have value for customers, clients, partners, and society at large. The term developed from the original meaning which referred literally to going to market, as in shopping, or going to a market to sell goods or services.

_____ practice tends to be seen as a creative industry, which includes advertising, distribution and selling.

a. Marketing
b. Product naming
c. Customer acquisition management
d. Marketing myopia

13. _____ was an abstract and index periodical and the print counterpart of the PsycINFO database. It was published by the American Psychological Association and was produced for 80 years, ceasing publication at the end of 2006. It was produced monthly and contained summaries (abstracts, bibliographic information, and indexing) of English-language journal articles, technical reports, book chapters, and books in the field of psychology.
a. 180SearchAssistant
b. Psychological Abstracts
c. Power III
d. Selective distortion

14. The _____ is an English-language international daily newspaper published by Dow Jones ' Company in New York City with Asian and European editions. As of 2007, It has a worldwide daily circulation of more than 2 million, with approximately 931,000 paying online subscribers. It was the largest-circulation newspaper in the United States until November 2003, when it was surpassed by USA Today.
a. Power III
b. 180SearchAssistant
c. 6-3-5 Brainwriting
d. Wall Street Journal

Chapter 5. Secondary Sources of Marketing Data   23

15. _____ is a form of direct marketing using databases of customers or potential customers to generate personalized communications in order to promote a product or service for marketing purposes. The method of communication can be any addressable medium, as in direct marketing.

The distinction between direct and _____ stems primarily from the attention paid to the analysis of data.

   a. Direct marketing   b. Power III
   c. Direct Marketing Associations   d. Database marketing

16. _____s is the social science that studies the production, distribution, and consumption of goods and services. The term _____s comes from the Ancient Greek oá¼°κονομῖα from oá¼¶κος (oikos, 'house') + vÏŒμος (nomos, 'custom' or 'law'), hence 'rules of the house(hold)'. Current _____ models developed out of the broader field of political economy in the late 19th century, owing to a desire to use an empirical approach more akin to the physical sciences.
   a. Economic   b. Industrial organization
   c. ADTECH   d. ACNielsen

17. A _____ is a type of wholesale merchant business that buys goods and bulk products from importers, other wholesalers and then sells to retailers. _____s can deal in any commodity destined for the retail market. Typical categories are food, lumber, hardware, fuel, and textiles.
   a. Tacit collusion   b. Refusal to deal
   c. Chief privacy officer   d. Jobbing house

18. The _____ is a publication of the United States Census Bureau, an agency of the United States Department of Commerce. Published annually since 1878, the statistics describe social and economic conditions in the United States.

In 1975 a two volume Historical Statistics of the United States, Colonial Times to 1970 Bicentennial Edition was published.

   a. 6-3-5 Brainwriting   b. Power III
   c. Statistical Abstract of the United States d. 180SearchAssistant

19. The _____ of American Manufacturers is a multi-volume directory of industrial product information covering 650,000 distributors, manufacturers and service companies within 67,000-plus industrial categories. It was first published in 1898 by Harvey Mark Thomas as Hardware and Kindred Trades. The company stopped publishing its print products in 2006 due to declining circulation as Internet searches eroded the products' usability.
   a. Stock management   b. Futura plus
   c. Free box   d. Thomas Register

20. A bibliographic or library database is a database of bibliographic records. It may be a database containing information about books and other materials held in a library (e.g. an online library catalog, or OPAC) or, as the term is more often used, an electronic index to journal or magazine articles, containing citations, abstracts and often either the full text of the articles indexed, or links to the full text.

Many scientific databases are _____, but some are not.

a. 6-3-5 Brainwriting
c. 180SearchAssistant
b. Power III
d. Bibliographic databases

21. _____ is an advertisement in which a particular product specifically mentions a competitor by name for the express purpose of showing why the competitor is inferior to the product naming it.

This should not be confused with parody advertisements, where a fictional product is being advertised for the purpose of poking fun at the particular advertisement, nor should it be confused with the use of a coined brand name for the purpose of comparing the product without actually naming an actual competitor. ('Wikipedia tastes better and is less filling than the Encyclopedia Galactica.')

In the 1980s, during what has been referred to as the cola wars, soft-drink manufacturer Pepsi ran a series of advertisements where people, caught on hidden camera, in a blind taste test, chose Pepsi over rival Coca-Cola.

a. GL-70
c. Cost per conversion
b. Heavy-up
d. Comparative advertising

22. _____ is the generic term for a class of software music sequencers which, in their purest form, allow the user to arrange sound samples stepwise on a timeline across several monophonic channels. A _____'s interface is primarily numeric; notes are entered via the alphanumeric keys of the computer keyboard, while parameters, effects and so forth are entered in hexadecimal. A complete song consists of several small multi-channel patterns chained together via a master list.

a. 180SearchAssistant
c. Power III
b. 6-3-5 Brainwriting
d. Tracker

23. A personal and cultural _____ is a relative ethic _____, an assumption upon which implementation can be extrapolated. A _____ system is a set of consistent _____s and measures that is soo not true. A principle _____ is a foundation upon which other _____s and measures of integrity are based.

a. Supreme Court of the United States
c. Perceptual maps
b. Package-on-Package
d. Value

24. _____ is a technology which allows a user to interact with a computer-simulated environment, whether that environment is a simulation of the real world or an imaginary world. Most current _____ environments are primarily visual experiences, displayed either on a computer screen or through special or stereoscopic displays, but some simulations include additional sensory information, such as sound through speakers or headphones. Some advanced, haptic systems now include tactile information, generally known as force feedback, in medical and gaming applications.

a. 6-3-5 Brainwriting
c. Virtual reality
b. 180SearchAssistant
d. Power III

25. _____ is the study of the Earth and its lands, features, inhabitants, and phenomena. A literal translation would be 'to describe or write about the Earth'. The first person to use the word '_____' was Eratosthenes .

a. 6-3-5 Brainwriting
c. Power III
b. 180SearchAssistant
d. Geography

Chapter 5. Secondary Sources of Marketing Data

26. In the United States, the Office of Management and Budget (OMB) has produced a formal definition of metropolitan areas. These are referred to as '_____s' (_____s) and 'Combined Statistical Areas.' An earlier version of the _____ was the 'Standard _____' (SMetropolitan statistical area.) _____s are composed of counties and for some county equivalents.
    a. Race and ethnicity in the United States Census
    b. Power III
    c. 180SearchAssistant
    d. Metropolitan statistical area

27. In economics, _____ is the desire to own something and the ability to pay for it. The term _____ signifies the ability or the willingness to buy a particular commodity at a given point of time.

    a. Market system
    b. Discretionary spending
    c. Market dominance
    d. Demand

28. _____ is the process of finding associated geographic coordinates (often expressed as latitude and longitude) from other geographic data, such as street addresses or the coordinates can be embedded into media such as digital photographs via geotagging.

    Reverse _____ is the opposite: finding an associated textual location such as a street address, from geographic coordinates.

    a. Geocoding
    b. 180SearchAssistant
    c. Power III
    d. 6-3-5 Brainwriting

29. _____ is a type of advertising whereby advertisements are placed so as to reach consumers based on various traits such as demographics, purchase history, or observed behavior.

    Two principal forms of targeted interactive advertising are behavioral targeting and contextual advertising.

    a. Brand parity
    b. Sugging
    c. Specialty catalogs
    d. Targeted advertising

30. _____ is a form of marketing developed from direct response marketing campaigns conducted in the 1970's and 1980's which emphasizes customer retention and satisfaction, rather than a dominant focus on 'point of sale' transactions.

    _____ differs from other forms of marketing in that it recognizes the long term value to the firm of keeping customers, as opposed to direct or 'Intrusion' marketing, which focuses upon acquisition of new clients by targeting majority demographics based upon prospective client lists.

    _____ refers to long-term and mutually beneficial arrangement wherein both buyer and seller focus on value enhancement through the certain of more satisfying exchange. This approach attempts to transcend the simple purchase exchange process with customer to make more meaningful and richer contact by providing a more holistic, personalized purchase, and use orn consumption experience to create stronger ties.

a. Global marketing
c. Diversity marketing
b. Relationship marketing
d. Guerrilla Marketing

31. Consumer market research is a form of applied sociology that concentrates on understanding the behaviours, whims and preferences, of consumers in a market-based economy, and aims to understand the effects and comparative success of marketing campaigns. The field of consumer _____ as a statistical science was pioneered by Arthur Nielsen with the founding of the ACNielsen Company in 1923.

Thus _____ is the systematic and objective identification, collection, analysis, and dissemination of information for the purpose of assisting management in decision making related to the identification and solution of problems and opportunities in marketing.

a. Marketing research
c. Marketing research process
b. Focus group
d. Logit analysis

32. _____ in statistics and econometrics is a type of one-dimensional data set. _____ refers to data collected by observing many subjects (such as individuals, firms or countries/regions) at the same point of time, or without regard to differences in time. Analysis of _____ usually consists of comparing the differences among the subjects.

a. Descriptive research
c. Two-tailed test
b. Sampling error
d. Cross-sectional data

33. _____ is the process of estimation in unknown situations. Prediction is a similar, but more general term. Both can refer to estimation of time series, cross-sectional or longitudinal data.

a. 180SearchAssistant
c. Forecasting
b. Power III
d. 6-3-5 Brainwriting

Chapter 6. Standardized Sources of Marketing Data

1. The general definition of an _____ is an evaluation of a person, organization, system, process, project or product. _____s are performed to ascertain the validity and reliability of information; also to provide an assessment of a system's internal control. The goal of an _____ is to express an opinion on the person/organization/system (etc) in question, under evaluation based on work done on a test basis.
   - a. ACNielsen
   - b. AMAX
   - c. ADTECH
   - d. Audit

2. _____ is a radio audience research company in the United States which collects listener data on radio audiences similar to that collected by Nielsen Media Research on television audiences. It was founded as American Research Bureau by Jim Seiler in 1949 and became bi-coastal by merging with L.A. based Coffin, Cooper and Clay in the early 1950s. ARB's initial business was the collection of television broadcast ratings exclusively.
   - a. American Cancer Society
   - b. American Heart Association
   - c. Arbitron
   - d. Access Commerce

3. _____ is a broad label that refers to any individuals or households that use goods and services generated within the economy. The concept of a _____ is used in different contexts, so that the usage and significance of the term may vary.

   A _____ is a person who uses any product or service.

   - a. Consumer
   - b. 6-3-5 Brainwriting
   - c. Power III
   - d. 180SearchAssistant

4. _____ is an advertisement in which a particular product specifically mentions a competitor by name for the express purpose of showing why the competitor is inferior to the product naming it.

   This should not be confused with parody advertisements, where a fictional product is being advertised for the purpose of poking fun at the particular advertisement, nor should it be confused with the use of a coined brand name for the purpose of comparing the product without actually naming an actual competitor. ('Wikipedia tastes better and is less filling than the Encyclopedia Galactica.')

   In the 1980s, during what has been referred to as the cola wars, soft-drink manufacturer Pepsi ran a series of advertisements where people, caught on hidden camera, in a blind taste test, chose Pepsi over rival Coca-Cola.

   - a. Cost per conversion
   - b. Heavy-up
   - c. GL-70
   - d. Comparative advertising

5. _____ is one of the four growth strategies of the Product-Market Growth Matrix defined by Ansoff. _____ occurs when a company enters/penetrates a market with current products. The best way to achieve this is by gaining competitors' customers (part of their market share.)
   - a. Pasar pagi
   - b. Marketization
   - c. Horizontal market
   - d. Market penetration

6. _____ is a distortion of evidence or data that arises from the way that the data are collected. It is sometimes referred to as the selection effect. The term _____ most often refers to the distortion of a statistical analysis, due to the method of collecting samples.

a. Selection bias
c. Systematic sampling
b. 180SearchAssistant
d. Power III

7. _____ is a standard point of view or personal prejudice. especially when the tendency interferes with the ability to be impartial, unprejudiced, or objective. The term _____ed is used to describe an action, judgment, or other outcome influenced by a prejudged perspective.
   a. Power III
   b. Bias
   c. 180SearchAssistant
   d. 6-3-5 Brainwriting

8. _____ refer to a collection of facts usually collected as the result of experience, observation or experiment or a set of premises. This may consist of numbers, words particularly as measurements or observations of a set of variables. _____ are often viewed as a lowest level of abstraction from which information and knowledge are derived.
   a. Sample size
   b. Pearson product-moment correlation coefficient
   c. Data
   d. Mean

9. _____ is defined by the American _____ Association as the activity, set of institutions, and processes for creating, communicating, delivering, and exchanging offerings that have value for customers, clients, partners, and society at large. The term developed from the original meaning which referred literally to going to market, as in shopping, or going to a market to sell goods or services.

_____ practice tends to be seen as a creative industry, which includes advertising, distribution and selling.

   a. Customer acquisition management
   b. Product naming
   c. Marketing
   d. Marketing myopia

10. Consumer market research is a form of applied sociology that concentrates on understanding the behaviours, whims and preferences, of consumers in a market-based economy, and aims to understand the effects and comparative success of marketing campaigns. The field of consumer _____ as a statistical science was pioneered by Arthur Nielsen with the founding of the ACNielsen Company in 1923 .

Thus _____ is the systematic and objective identification, collection, analysis, and dissemination of information for the purpose of assisting management in decision making related to the identification and solution of problems and opportunities in marketing.

   a. Focus group
   b. Marketing research process
   c. Logit analysis
   d. Marketing Research

11. A _____ is an optical machine-readable representation of data. Originally, _____s represented data in the widths (lines) and the spacings of parallel lines and may be referred to as linear or 1D (1 dimensional) barcodes or symbologies. But they also come in patterns of squares, dots, hexagons and other geometric patterns within images termed 2D (2 dimensional) matrix codes or symbologies.
   a. 6-3-5 Brainwriting
   b. 180SearchAssistant
   c. Power III
   d. Bar code

12. Electronic commerce, commonly known as _____ or eCommerce, consists of the buying and selling of products or services over electronic systems such as the Internet and other computer networks. The amount of trade conducted electronically has grown extraordinarily with wide-spread Internet usage. A wide variety of commerce is conducted in this way, spurring and drawing on innovations in electronic funds transfer, supply chain management, Internet marketing, online transaction processing, electronic data interchange (EDI), inventory management systems, and automated data collection systems.

a. AMAX
b. ADTECH
c. ACNielsen
d. E-commerce

13. _____ is a form of communication that typically attempts to persuade potential customers to purchase or to consume more of a particular brand of product or service. 'While now central to the contemporary global economy and the reproduction of global production networks, it is only quite recently that _____ has been more than a marginal influence on patterns of sales and production. The formation of modern _____ was intimately bound up with the emergence of new forms of monopoly capitalism around the end of the 19th and beginning of the 20th century as one element in corporate strategies to create, organize and where possible control markets, especially for mass produced consumer goods.

a. Advertising
b. ACNielsen
c. AMAX
d. ADTECH

14. Human beings are also considered to be _____ because they have the ability to change raw materials into valuable _____. The term Human _____ can also be defined as the skills, energies, talents, abilities and knowledge that are used for the production of goods or the rendering of services. While taking into account human beings as _____, the following things have to be kept in mind:

- The size of the population
- The capabilities of the individuals in that population

Many _____ cannot be consumed in their original form. They have to be processed in order to change them into more usable commodities.

a. 180SearchAssistant
b. 6-3-5 Brainwriting
c. Power III
d. Resources

15. _____ involves disseminating information about a product, product line, brand, or company. It is one of the four key aspects of the marketing mix. (The other three elements are product marketing, pricing, and distribution). P>_____ is generally sub-divided into two parts:

- Above the line _____: Promotion in the media (e.g. TV, radio, newspapers, Internet and Mobile Phones) in which the advertiser pays an advertising agency to place the ad
- Below the line _____: All other _____. Much of this is intended to be subtle enough for the consumer to be unaware that _____ is taking place. E.g. sponsorship, product placement, endorsements, sales _____, merchandising, direct mail, personal selling, public relations, trade shows

a. Cashmere Agency
b. Bottling lines
c. Promotion
d. Davie Brown Index

Chapter 6. Standardized Sources of Marketing Data

16. _____ is an American firm that measures media audiences, including television, radio, theatre films (via the AMC MAP program) and newspapers. _____, headquartered in New York City and operating primarily from Chicago, is best-known for the Nielsen Ratings, a measurement of television viewership.

_____, the preeminent media research company in the world, began as a division of ACNielsen, a marketing research firm.

a. Nielsen Media Research
b. Hennes ' Mauritz
c. Green Earth Market
d. CoolBrands

17. _____ describes data and characteristics about the population or phenomenon being studied. _____ answers the questions who, what, where, when and how.

Although the data description is factual, accurate and systematic, the research cannot describe what caused a situation.

a. Two-tailed test
b. Sampling error
c. Power III
d. Descriptive research

18. A _____ is a tool used to measure the viewing habits of TV and cable audiences.

The _____ is a 'box', about the size of a paperback book. The box is hooked up to each television set and is accompanied by a remote control unit.

a. 180SearchAssistant
b. 6-3-5 Brainwriting
c. Power III
d. People Meter

19. In economics, _____ is the desire to own something and the ability to pay for it. The term _____ signifies the ability or the willingness to buy a particular commodity at a given point of time .

a. Market dominance
b. Market system
c. Discretionary spending
d. Demand

20. _____, in strategic management and marketing, is the percentage or proportion of the total available market or market segment that is being serviced by a company. It can be expressed as a company's sales revenue (from that market) divided by the total sales revenue available in that market. It can also be expressed as a company's unit sales volume (in a market) divided by the total volume of units sold in that market.

a. Customer relationship management
b. Market share
c. Cyberdoc
d. Demand generation

21. Competitiveness is a comparative concept of the ability and performance of a firm, sub-sector or country to sell and supply goods and/or services in a given market. Although widely used in economics and business management, the usefulness of the concept, particularly in the context of national competitiveness, is vigorously disputed by economists, such as Paul Krugman .

Chapter 6. Standardized Sources of Marketing Data 31

The term may also be applied to markets, where it is used to refer to the extent to which the market structure may be regarded as perfectly _____.

a. Free trade zone
b. Customs union
c. Geographical pricing
d. Competitive

22. _____ is, in very basic words, a position a firm occupies against its competitors.

According to Michael Porter, the three methods for creating a sustainable _____ are through:

1. Cost leadership - Cost advantage occurs when a firm delivers the same services as its competitors but at a lower cost;

2.

a. Power III
b. 180SearchAssistant
c. Competitive advantage
d. 6-3-5 Brainwriting

23. An _____ is the manufacturing of a good or service within a category. Although _____ is a broad term for any kind of economic production, in economics and urban planning _____ is a synonym for the secondary sector, which is a type of economic activity involved in the manufacturing of raw materials into goods and products.

There are four key industrial economic sectors: the primary sector, largely raw material extraction industries such as mining and farming; the secondary sector, involving refining, construction, and manufacturing; the tertiary sector, which deals with services (such as law and medicine) and distribution of manufactured goods; and the quaternary sector, a relatively new type of knowledge _____ focusing on technological research, design and development such as computer programming, and biochemistry.

a. ADTECH
b. Industry
c. AMAX
d. ACNielsen

24. The _____ or _____ is used by business and government to classify and measure economic activity in Canada, Mexico and the United States. It has largely replaced the older Standard Industrial Classification system; however, certain government departments and agencies, such as the U.S. Securities and Exchange Commission (SEC), still use the SIC codes.

The _____ numbering system is a six-digit code.

a. 180SearchAssistant
b. North American Industry Classification System
c. Power III
d. 6-3-5 Brainwriting

25. _____ is systematic determination of merit, worth, and significance of something or someone using criteria against a set of standards. _____ often is used to characterize and appraise subjects of interest in a wide range of human enterprises, including the arts, criminal justice, foundations and non-profit organizations, government, health care, and other human services.

Depending on the topic of interest, there are professional groups which look to the quality and rigor of the _____ process.

a. ADTECH
c. AMAX
b. ACNielsen
d. Evaluation

Chapter 7. Marketing Research on the Internet

1. Electronic commerce, commonly known as _____ or eCommerce, consists of the buying and selling of products or services over electronic systems such as the Internet and other computer networks. The amount of trade conducted electronically has grown extraordinarily with wide-spread Internet usage. A wide variety of commerce is conducted in this way, spurring and drawing on innovations in electronic funds transfer, supply chain management, Internet marketing, online transaction processing, electronic data interchange (EDI), inventory management systems, and automated data collection systems.

   a. ADTECH
   b. E-commerce
   c. ACNielsen
   d. AMAX

2. _____ is the examining of goods or services from retailers with the intent to purchase at that time. _____ is an activity of selection and/or purchase. In some contexts it is considered a leisure activity as well as an economic one.

   a. Khodebshchik
   b. Discount store
   c. Hawkers
   d. Shopping

3. _____ is defined by the American _____ Association as the activity, set of institutions, and processes for creating, communicating, delivering, and exchanging offerings that have value for customers, clients, partners, and society at large. The term developed from the original meaning which referred literally to going to market, as in shopping, or going to a market to sell goods or services.

   _____ practice tends to be seen as a creative industry, which includes advertising, distribution and selling.

   a. Customer acquisition management
   b. Product naming
   c. Marketing myopia
   d. Marketing

4. A _____, in the field of business and marketing, is a geographic region or demographic group used to gauge the viability of a product or service in the mass market prior to a wide scale roll-out. The criteria used to judge the acceptability of a _____ region or group include:

   1. a population that is demographically similar to the proposed target market; and
   2. relative isolation from densely populated media markets so that advertising to the test audience can be efficient and economical.

The _____ ideally aims to duplicate 'everything' - promotion and distribution as well as `product' - on a smaller scale. The technique replicates, typically in one area, what is planned to occur in a national launch; and the results are very carefully monitored, so that they can be extrapolated to projected national results. The `area' may be any one of the following:

- Television area
- Test town
- Residential neighborhood
- Test site

Chapter 7. Marketing Research on the Internet

A number of decisions have to be taken about any _____:

- Which _____?
- What is to be tested?
- How long a test?
- What are the success criteria?

The simple go or no-go decision, together with the related reduction of risk, is normally the main justification for the expense of _____s. At the same time, however, such _____s can be used to test specific elements of a new product's marketing mix; possibly the version of the product itself, the promotional message and media spend, the distribution channels and the price.

a. Preadolescence
b. Test market
c. 180SearchAssistant
d. Power III

5. _____ is a form of communication that typically attempts to persuade potential customers to purchase or to consume more of a particular brand of product or service. 'While now central to the contemporary global economy and the reproduction of global production networks, it is only quite recently that _____ has been more than a marginal influence on patterns of sales and production. The formation of modern _____ was intimately bound up with the emergence of new forms of monopoly capitalism around the end of the 19th and beginning of the 20th century as one element in corporate strategies to create, organize and where possible control markets, especially for mass produced consumer goods.

a. ACNielsen
b. Advertising
c. AMAX
d. ADTECH

6. _____ is a form of promotion that uses the Internet and World Wide Web for the expressed purpose of delivering marketing messages to attract customers. Examples of _____ include contextual ads on search engine results pages, banner ads, Rich Media Ads, Social network advertising, online classified advertising, advertising networks and e-mail marketing, including e-mail spam.

Online video directories for brands are a good example of interactive advertising.

a. ACNielsen
b. AMAX
c. Online Advertising
d. ADTECH

7. _____ is a form of targeted advertising for advertisements appearing on websites or other media, such as content displayed in mobile browsers. The advertisements themselves are selected and served by automated systems based on the content displayed to the user.

A _____ system scans the text of a website for keywords and returns advertisements to the webpage based on what the user is viewing.

a. Click-through rate
b. Click fraud
c. Multivariate testing
d. Contextual advertising

8. _____ is a broad label that refers to any individuals or households that use goods and services generated within the economy. The concept of a _____ is used in different contexts, so that the usage and significance of the term may vary.

A _____ is a person who uses any product or service.

a. Consumer
b. 180SearchAssistant
c. Power III
d. 6-3-5 Brainwriting

9. _____ is an independent technology and market research company that provides its clients with advice about technology's impact on business and consumers. _____ has four research centers in the US: Cambridge, Massachusetts; Foster City, California; Washington, D.C.; and Westport, Connecticut. It also has four European research centers in Amsterdam, Frankfurt, London, and Paris.

a. GlobalSpec
b. BigMachines
c. Mapinfo
d. Forrester Research

10. _____ is an advertisement in which a particular product specifically mentions a competitor by name for the express purpose of showing why the competitor is inferior to the product naming it.

This should not be confused with parody advertisements, where a fictional product is being advertised for the purpose of poking fun at the particular advertisement, nor should it be confused with the use of a coined brand name for the purpose of comparing the product without actually naming an actual competitor. ('Wikipedia tastes better and is less filling than the Encyclopedia Galactica.')

In the 1980s, during what has been referred to as the cola wars, soft-drink manufacturer Pepsi ran a series of advertisements where people, caught on hidden camera, in a blind taste test, chose Pepsi over rival Coca-Cola.

a. GL-70
b. Cost per conversion
c. Heavy-up
d. Comparative advertising

11. A _____ is a collection of symbols, experiences and associations connected with a product, a service, a person or any other artifact or entity.

_____s have become increasingly important components of culture and the economy, now being described as 'cultural accessories and personal philosophies'.

Some people distinguish the psychological aspect of a _____ from the experiential aspect.

a. Brand equity
b. Brandable software
c. Store brand
d. Brand

12. _____ refers to the marketing effects or outcomes that accrue to a product with its brand name compared with those that would accrue if the same product did not have the brand name . And, at the root of these marketing effects is consumers' knowledge. In other words, consumers' knowledge about a brand makes manufacturers/advertisers respond differently or adopt appropriately adapt measures for the marketing of the brand .

a. Product extension
b. Brand image
c. Brand aversion
d. Brand equity

13. _____ involves the collection of data that does not already exist. This can be through numerous forms, including questionnaires and telephone interviews amongst others. This information may be collected in things like questionnaires, magazines, and Interviews

The term is widely used in market research and competitive intelligence.

a. Bitcom
b. Primary research
c. Brand infiltration
d. Blitz QFD

14. _____ are used to collect quantitative information about items in a population. Surveys of human populations and institutions are common in political polling and government, health, social science and marketing research. A survey may focus on opinions or factual information depending on its purpose, and many surveys involve administering questions to individuals.

a. Statistical surveys
b. BeyondROI
c. Convergent
d. Gross Margin Return on Inventory Investment

15. A _____ is a form of qualitative research in which a group of people are asked about their attitude towards a product, service, concept, advertisement, idea, or packaging. Questions are asked in an interactive group setting where participants are free to talk with other group members.

Ernest Dichter originated the idea of having a 'group therapy' for products and this process is what became known as a _____.

a. Cross tabulation
b. Focus group
c. Logit analysis
d. Marketing research process

16. An _____ is one type of focus group, and is a sub-set of online research methods.

A moderator invites prescreened, qualified respondents who represent the target of interest to log on to conferencing software at a pre-arranged time and to take part in an _____. Some researchers will offer incentives for participating but this raises a number of ethical questions.

a. Online Focus group
b. Intangibility
c. Automated surveys
d. Engagement

17. _____ involves the summary, collation and/or synthesis of existing research rather than primary research, where data is collected from, for example, research subjects or experiments.

The term is widely used in market research and in medical research. The principal methodology in medical _____ is the systematic review, commonly using meta-analytic statistical techniques, although other methods of synthesis, like realist reviews and meta-narrative reviews, have been developed in recent years.

Chapter 7. Marketing Research on the Internet

a. 180SearchAssistant
b. Secondary research
c. 6-3-5 Brainwriting
d. Power III

18. A supply chain is the system of organizations, people, technology, activities, information and resources involved in moving a product or service from _____ to customer. Supply chain activities transform natural resources, raw materials and components into a finished product that is delivered to the end customer. In sophisticated supply chain systems, used products may re-enter the supply chain at any point where residual value is recyclable.
    a. Supplier
    b. Bringin' Home the Oil
    c. Rebate
    d. Product line extension

19. In artificial intelligence, an _____ is an autonomous entity which observes and acts upon an environment (i.e. it is an agent) and directs its activity towards achieving goals (i.e. it is rational.) _____s may also learn or use knowledge to achieve their goals. They may be very simple or very complex: a reflex machine such as a thermostat is an _____, as is a human being, as is a community of human beings working together towards a goal.
    a. ACNielsen
    b. AMAX
    c. Intelligent agent
    d. ADTECH

20. Consumer market research is a form of applied sociology that concentrates on understanding the behaviours, whims and preferences, of consumers in a market-based economy, and aims to understand the effects and comparative success of marketing campaigns. The field of consumer _____ as a statistical science was pioneered by Arthur Nielsen with the founding of the ACNielsen Company in 1923 .

Thus _____ is the systematic and objective identification, collection, analysis, and dissemination of information for the purpose of assisting management in decision making related to the identification and solution of problems and opportunities in marketing.

   a. Focus group
   b. Marketing research
   c. Marketing research process
   d. Logit analysis

21. _____ is a sales technique in which a salesperson walks from one door of a house to another trying to sell a product or service to the general public. A variant of this involves cold calling first, when another sales representative attempts to gain agreement that a salesperson should visit. _____ selling is usually conducted in the afternoon hours, when the majority of people are at home.
    a. Marketing management
    b. Fast moving consumer goods
    c. Door-to-door
    d. Performance-based advertising

22. _____ is that part of statistical practice concerned with the selection of individual observations intended to yield some knowledge about a population of concern, especially for the purposes of statistical inference. Each observation measures one or more properties (weight, location, etc.) of an observable entity enumerated to distinguish objects or individuals.
    a. Sports Marketing Group
    b. AStore
    c. Richard Buckminster 'Bucky' Fuller
    d. Sampling

Chapter 7. Marketing Research on the Internet

23. _____ is a crime used to refer to fraud that involves someone pretending to be someone else in order to steal money or get other benefits. The term is relatively new and is actually a misnomer, since it is not inherently possible to steal an identity, only to use it. The person whose identity is used can suffer various consequences when he or she is held responsible for the perpetrator's actions.
   a. ADTECH
   b. ACNielsen
   c. AMAX
   d. Identity theft

24. _____ is the ability of an individual or group to seclude themselves or information about themselves and thereby reveal themselves selectively. The boundaries and content of what is considered private differ among cultures and individuals, but share basic common themes. _____ is sometimes related to anonymity, the wish to remain unnoticed or unidentified in the public realm.
   a. 180SearchAssistant
   b. 6-3-5 Brainwriting
   c. Power III
   d. Privacy

Chapter 8. Information Collection

1. _____ is a field of inquiry that crosscuts disciplines and subject matters . _____ers aim to gather an in-depth understanding of human behavior and the reasons that govern such behavior. The discipline investigates the why and how of decision making, not just what, where, when.
   a. Power III
   b. Qualitative research
   c. 6-3-5 Brainwriting
   d. 180SearchAssistant

2. _____ is a sales technique in which a salesperson walks from one door of a house to another trying to sell a product or service to the general public. A variant of this involves cold calling first, when another sales representative attempts to gain agreement that a salesperson should visit. _____ selling is usually conducted in the afternoon hours, when the majority of people are at home.
   a. Marketing management
   b. Fast moving consumer goods
   c. Performance-based advertising
   d. Door-to-door

3. _____ is an investment technique that requires investors to purchase multiple financial products with different maturity dates.

   _____ avoids the risk of reinvesting a big portion of assets in an unfavorable financial environment. For example, a person has both a 2015 matured CD and a 2018 matured CD.

   a. Laddering
   b. 180SearchAssistant
   c. 6-3-5 Brainwriting
   d. Power III

4. _____ is a metatheory, which is used for interpreting relations between symbols. It can be made either manually or by using computer tools.

   All languages are made up of symbols.

   a. Power III
   b. Graphic communication
   c. Public relations
   d. Symbolic analysis

5. A _____ is a form of qualitative research in which a group of people are asked about their attitude towards a product, service, concept, advertisement, idea, or packaging. Questions are asked in an interactive group setting where participants are free to talk with other group members.

   Ernest Dichter originated the idea of having a 'group therapy' for products and this process is what became known as a _____.

   a. Logit analysis
   b. Marketing research process
   c. Cross tabulation
   d. Focus group

6. _____ in organizations and public policy is both the organizational process of creating and maintaining a plan; and the psychological process of thinking about the activities required to create a desired goal on some scale. As such, it is a fundamental property of intelligent behavior. This thought process is essential to the creation and refinement of a plan, or integration of it with other plans, that is, it combines forecasting of developments with the preparation of scenarios of how to react to them.

Chapter 8. Information Collection

a. Planning
b. Power III
c. 6-3-5 Brainwriting
d. 180SearchAssistant

7. Procter is a surname, and may also refer to:

- Bryan Waller Procter (pseud. Barry Cornwall), English poet
- Goodwin Procter, American law firm
- _____, consumer products multinational

a. Convergent
b. Black PRies
c. Procter ' Gamble
d. Flyer

8. An _____ is one type of focus group, and is a sub-set of online research methods.

A moderator invites prescreened, qualified respondents who represent the target of interest to log on to conferencing software at a pre-arranged time and to take part in an _____. Some researchers will offer incentives for participating but this raises a number of ethical questions.

a. Automated surveys
b. Intangibility
c. Online Focus group
d. Engagement

9. The _____ is an example of a projective test.

Historically, the _____ or _____ has been amongst the most widely used, researched, and taught projective psychological tests. Its adherents claim that it taps a subject's unconscious to reveal repressed aspects of personality, motives and needs for achievement, power and intimacy, and problem-solving abilities.

a. Thematic Apperception Test
b. Power III
c. 6-3-5 Brainwriting
d. 180SearchAssistant

10. _____ is the realization of an application idea, model, design, specification, standard, algorithm an _____ is a realization of a technical specification or algorithm as a program, software component, or other computer system. Many _____s may exist for a given specification or standard.

a. ACNielsen
b. ADTECH
c. AMAX
d. Implementation

11. _____ is either an activity of a living being (such as a human), consisting of receiving knowledge of the outside world through the senses, or the recording of data using scientific instruments. The term may also refer to any datum collected during this activity.

The scientific method requires _____s of nature to formulate and test hypotheses.

a. ACNielsen
b. AMAX
c. ADTECH
d. Observation

Chapter 8. Information Collection

12. _____ is a methodology in the social sciences for studying the content of communication. Earl Babbie defines it as 'the study of recorded human communications, such as books, websites, paintings and laws.' It is most commonly used by researchers in the social sciences to analyze recorded transcripts of interviews with participants.

_____ is also considered a scholarly methodology in the humanities by which texts are studied as to authorship, authenticity, of meaning.

- a. Content analysis
- b. 180SearchAssistant
- c. Power III
- d. 6-3-5 Brainwriting

13. The general definition of an _____ is an evaluation of a person, organization, system, process, project or product. _____s are performed to ascertain the validity and reliability of information; also to provide an assessment of a system's internal control. The goal of an _____ is to express an opinion on the person/organization/system (etc) in question, under evaluation based on work done on a test basis.
- a. AMAX
- b. ADTECH
- c. ACNielsen
- d. Audit

14. A _____ is a tool used to measure the viewing habits of TV and cable audiences.

The _____ is a 'box', about the size of a paperback book. The box is hooked up to each television set and is accompanied by a remote control unit.

- a. 180SearchAssistant
- b. Power III
- c. 6-3-5 Brainwriting
- d. People Meter

15. _____ refer to a collection of facts usually collected as the result of experience, observation or experiment or a set of premises. This may consist of numbers, words particularly as measurements or observations of a set of variables. _____ are often viewed as a lowest level of abstraction from which information and knowledge are derived.
- a. Sample size
- b. Mean
- c. Pearson product-moment correlation coefficient
- d. Data

16. A _____ applies the scientific method to experimentally examine an intervention in the real world (or as many experimental economists like to say, naturally-occurring environments) rather than in the laboratory. _____s, like lab experiments, generally randomize subjects (or other sampling units) into treatment and control groups and compare outcomes between these groups. Clinical trials of pharmaceuticals are one example of _____s.
- a. Response variable
- b. Power III
- c. 180SearchAssistant
- d. Field experiment

17. _____ is defined by the American _____ Association as the activity, set of institutions, and processes for creating, communicating, delivering, and exchanging offerings that have value for customers, clients, partners, and society at large. The term developed from the original meaning which referred literally to going to market, as in shopping, or going to a market to sell goods or services.

_____ practice tends to be seen as a creative industry, which includes advertising, distribution and selling.

a. Marketing
b. Marketing myopia
c. Customer acquisition management
d. Product naming

18. Consumer market research is a form of applied sociology that concentrates on understanding the behaviours, whims and preferences, of consumers in a market-based economy, and aims to understand the effects and comparative success of marketing campaigns. The field of consumer _____ as a statistical science was pioneered by Arthur Nielsen with the founding of the ACNielsen Company in 1923.

Thus _____ is the systematic and objective identification, collection, analysis, and dissemination of information for the purpose of assisting management in decision making related to the identification and solution of problems and opportunities in marketing.

a. Logit analysis
b. Marketing Research
c. Focus group
d. Marketing research process

Chapter 9. Information from Respondents: Issues in Data Collection

1. _____ refer to a collection of facts usually collected as the result of experience, observation or experiment or a set of premises. This may consist of numbers, words particularly as measurements or observations of a set of variables. _____ are often viewed as a lowest level of abstraction from which information and knowledge are derived.
   - a. Mean
   - b. Data
   - c. Sample size
   - d. Pearson product-moment correlation coefficient

2. _____ is the area of law concerned with the protection and preservation of the privacy rights of individuals. Increasingly, governments and other public as well as private organizations collect vast amounts of personal information about individuals for a variety of purposes. The law of privacy regulates the type of information which may be collected and how this information may be used.
   - a. Collective mark
   - b. Madrid system
   - c. Trademark attorney
   - d. Privacy law

3. _____ is a standard point of view or personal prejudice. especially when the tendency interferes with the ability to be impartial, unprejudiced, or objective. The term _____ed is used to describe an action, judgment, or other outcome influenced by a prejudged perspective.
   - a. Bias
   - b. Power III
   - c. 180SearchAssistant
   - d. 6-3-5 Brainwriting

4. _____ is the ability of an individual or group to seclude themselves or information about themselves and thereby reveal themselves selectively. The boundaries and content of what is considered private differ among cultures and individuals, but share basic common themes. _____ is sometimes related to anonymity, the wish to remain unnoticed or unidentified in the public realm.
   - a. 180SearchAssistant
   - b. 6-3-5 Brainwriting
   - c. Power III
   - d. Privacy

5. _____ is a type of cognitive bias which can affect the results of a statistical survey if respondents answer questions in the way they think the questioner wants them to answer rather than according to their true beliefs. This may occur if the questioner is obviously angling for a particular answer (as in push polling) or if the respondent wishes to please the questioner by answering what appears to be the 'morally right' answer. An example of the latter might be if a woman surveys a man on his attitudes to domestic violence, or someone who obviously cares about the environment asks people how much they value a wilderness area.
   - a. Von Restorff effect
   - b. Response bias
   - c. Power III
   - d. 180SearchAssistant

6. _____ is a term used to describe a process of preparing and collecting data - for example as part of a process improvement or similar project.

_____ usually takes place early on in an improvement project, and is often formalised through a _____ Plan which often contains the following activity.

   1. Pre collection activity - Agree goals, target data, definitions, methods
   2. Collection - _____
   3. Present Findings - usually involves some form of sorting analysis and/or presentation.

Chapter 9. Information from Respondents: Issues in Data Collection

A formal _____ process is necessary as it ensures that data gathered is both defined and accurate and that subsequent decisions based on arguments embodied in the findings are valid. The process provides both a baseline from which to measure from and in certain cases a target on what to improve. Types of _____ 1-By mail questionnaires 2-By personal interview

- Six sigma
- Sampling (statistics)

a. Data collection
c. Power III
b. 180SearchAssistant
d. 6-3-5 Brainwriting

7. The _____ of a statistical sample is the number of observations that constitute it. It is typically denoted n, a positive integer (natural number.)

Typically, all else being equal, a larger _____ leads to increased precision in estimates of various properties of the population.

a. Sample size
c. Frequency distribution
b. Data
d. Heteroskedastic

8. _____ is anything that is intended to save time, energy or frustration. A _____ store at a petrol station, for example, sells items that have nothing to do with gasoline/petrol, but it saves the consumer from having to go to a grocery store. '_____' is a very relative term and its meaning tends to change over time.

a. Marketing buzz
c. Demographic profile
b. MaxDiff
d. Convenience

9. _____ is a type of nonprobability sampling which involves the sample being drawn from that part of the population which is close to hand. That is, a sample population selected because it is readily available and convenient. The researcher using such a sample cannot scientifically make generalizations about the total population from this sample because it would not be representative enough.

a. Accidental sampling
c. ADTECH
b. AMAX
d. ACNielsen

10. In statistics, _____ has two related meanings:

- the arithmetic _____
- the expected value of a random variable, which is also called the population _____.

It is sometimes stated that the '_____' _____s average. This is incorrect if '_____' is taken in the specific sense of 'arithmetic _____' as there are different types of averages: the _____, median, and mode. For instance, average house prices almost always use the median value for the average. These three types of averages are all measures of locations.

a. Mean
b. Heteroskedastic
c. Confidence interval
d. Standard normal distribution

11. _____ is that part of statistical practice concerned with the selection of individual observations intended to yield some knowledge about a population of concern, especially for the purposes of statistical inference. Each observation measures one or more properties (weight, location, etc.) of an observable entity enumerated to distinguish objects or individuals.
a. AStore
b. Sports Marketing Group
c. Richard Buckminster 'Bucky' Fuller
d. Sampling

12. _____ in survey research refers to the ratio of number of people who answered the survey divided by the number of people in the sample. It is usually expressed in the form of a percentage.

Example: if 1,000 surveys were sent by mail, and 257 were successfully completed and returned, then the _____ would be 25.7 %.

a. Reference value
b. Sentence completion tests
c. Power III
d. Response rate

13. _____ generally refers to a list of all planned expenses and revenues. It is a plan for saving and spending. A _____ is an important concept in microeconomics, which uses a _____ line to illustrate the trade-offs between two or more goods.
a. 6-3-5 Brainwriting
b. Power III
c. Budget
d. 180SearchAssistant

14. In economics, business, retail, and accounting, a _____ is the value of money that has been used up to produce something, and hence is not available for use anymore. In economics, a _____ is an alternative that is given up as a result of a decision. In business, the _____ may be one of acquisition, in which case the amount of money expended to acquire it is counted as _____.
a. Transaction cost
b. Fixed costs
c. Variable cost
d. Cost

15. Competitiveness is a comparative concept of the ability and performance of a firm, sub-sector or country to sell and supply goods and/or services in a given market. Although widely used in economics and business management, the usefulness of the concept, particularly in the context of national competitiveness, is vigorously disputed by economists, such as Paul Krugman .

The term may also be applied to markets, where it is used to refer to the extent to which the market structure may be regarded as perfectly _____.

a. Customs union
b. Free trade zone
c. Geographical pricing
d. Competitive

16. _____ is, in very basic words, a position a firm occupies against its competitors.

According to Michael Porter, the three methods for creating a sustainable _____ are through:

1. Cost leadership - Cost advantage occurs when a firm delivers the same services as its competitors but at a lower cost;

2.

   a. 180SearchAssistant
   c. Power III
   b. 6-3-5 Brainwriting
   d. Competitive advantage

17. _____ is a branch of philosophy which seeks to address questions about morality, such as how a moral outcome can be achieved in a specific situation (applied _____), how moral values should be determined (normative _____), what moral values people actually abide by (descriptive _____), what the fundamental semantic, ontological, and epistemic nature of _____ or morality is (meta-_____), and how moral capacity or moral agency develops and what its nature is (moral psychology.)

Socrates was one of the first Greek philosophers to encourage both scholars and the common citizen to turn their attention from the outside world to the condition of man. In this view, Knowledge having a bearing on human life was placed highest, all other knowledge being secondary.

   a. ACNielsen
   c. ADTECH
   b. AMAX
   d. Ethics

18. The term _____ is primarily used by mass media to describe any form of synchronous conferencing, occasionally even asynchronous conferencing. The term can thus mean any technology ranging from real-time online chat over instant messaging and online forums to fully immersive graphical social environments.

Online chat is a way of communicating by sending text messages to people in the same chat-room in real-time.

   a. 180SearchAssistant
   c. Power III
   b. 6-3-5 Brainwriting
   d. Chat room

19. Electronic commerce, commonly known as _____ or eCommerce, consists of the buying and selling of products or services over electronic systems such as the Internet and other computer networks. The amount of trade conducted electronically has grown extraordinarily with wide-spread Internet usage. A wide variety of commerce is conducted in this way, spurring and drawing on innovations in electronic funds transfer, supply chain management, Internet marketing, online transaction processing, electronic data interchange (EDI), inventory management systems, and automated data collection systems.
   a. ACNielsen
   c. ADTECH
   b. AMAX
   d. E-commerce

Chapter 10. Information from Respondents: Survey Methods

1. _____ is a sales technique in which a salesperson walks from one door of a house to another trying to sell a product or service to the general public. A variant of this involves cold calling first, when another sales representative attempts to gain agreement that a salesperson should visit. _____ selling is usually conducted in the afternoon hours, when the majority of people are at home.
   - a. Fast moving consumer goods
   - b. Marketing management
   - c. Performance-based advertising
   - d. Door-to-door

2. A _____ is a research instrument consisting of a series of questions and other prompts for the purpose of gathering information from respondents. Although they are often designed for statistical analysis of the responses, this is not always the case. The _____ was invented by Sir Francis Galton.
   - a. Questionnaire
   - b. Mystery shoppers
   - c. Market research
   - d. Mystery shopping

3. In economics, business, retail, and accounting, a _____ is the value of money that has been used up to produce something, and hence is not available for use anymore. In economics, a _____ is an alternative that is given up as a result of a decision. In business, the _____ may be one of acquisition, in which case the amount of money expended to acquire it is counted as _____.
   - a. Variable cost
   - b. Cost
   - c. Transaction cost
   - d. Fixed costs

4. _____ is a standard point of view or personal prejudice. especially when the tendency interferes with the ability to be impartial, unprejudiced, or objective. The term _____ed is used to describe an action, judgment, or other outcome influenced by a prejudged perspective.
   - a. 180SearchAssistant
   - b. Power III
   - c. 6-3-5 Brainwriting
   - d. Bias

5. _____ is a branch of philosophy which seeks to address questions about morality, such as how a moral outcome can be achieved in a specific situation (applied _____), how moral values should be determined (normative _____), what moral values people actually abide by (descriptive _____), what the fundamental semantic, ontological, and epistemic nature of _____ or morality is (meta-_____), and how moral capacity or moral agency develops and what its nature is (moral psychology.)

Socrates was one of the first Greek philosophers to encourage both scholars and the common citizen to turn their attention from the outside world to the condition of man. In this view, Knowledge having a bearing on human life was placed highest, all other knowledge being secondary.

   - a. AMAX
   - b. Ethics
   - c. ACNielsen
   - d. ADTECH

6. _____ is defined by the American _____ Association as the activity, set of institutions, and processes for creating, communicating, delivering, and exchanging offerings that have value for customers, clients, partners, and society at large. The term developed from the original meaning which referred literally to going to market, as in shopping, or going to a market to sell goods or services.

_____ practice tends to be seen as a creative industry, which includes advertising, distribution and selling.

Chapter 10. Information from Respondents: Survey Methods

a. Marketing myopia
b. Product naming
c. Marketing
d. Customer acquisition management

7. A _____, in the field of business and marketing, is a geographic region or demographic group used to gauge the viability of a product or service in the mass market prior to a wide scale roll-out. The criteria used to judge the acceptability of a _____ region or group include:

1. a population that is demographically similar to the proposed target market; and
2. relative isolation from densely populated media markets so that advertising to the test audience can be efficient and economical.

The _____ ideally aims to duplicate 'everything' - promotion and distribution as well as `product' - on a smaller scale. The technique replicates, typically in one area, what is planned to occur in a national launch; and the results are very carefully monitored, so that they can be extrapolated to projected national results. The `area' may be any one of the following:

- Television area
- Test town
- Residential neighborhood
- Test site

A number of decisions have to be taken about any _____:

- Which _____?
- What is to be tested?
- How long a test?
- What are the success criteria?

The simple go or no-go decision, together with the related reduction of risk, is normally the main justification for the expense of _____s. At the same time, however, such _____s can be used to test specific elements of a new product's marketing mix; possibly the version of the product itself, the promotional message and media spend, the distribution channels and the price.

a. Preadolescence
b. Power III
c. 180SearchAssistant
d. Test market

8. _____ is a telephone surveying technique in which the interviewer follows a script provided by a software application. The software is able to customize the flow of the questionnaire based on the answers provided, as well as information already known about the participant.

CATI may function in the following manner

- A computerized questionnaire is administered to respondents over the telephone.
- The interviewer sits in front of a computer screen
- Upon command, the computer dials the telephone number to be called.
- When contact is made, the interviewer reads the questions posed on the computer screen and records the respondent's answers directly into the computer.
- Interim and update reports can be compiled instantaneously, as the data are being collected.
- CATI software has built-in logic, which also enhances data accuracy.
- The program will personalize questions and control for logically incorrect answers, such as percentage answers that do not add up to 100 percent.
- The software has built-in branching logic, which will skip questions that are not applicable or will probe for more detail when warranted.

a. 6-3-5 Brainwriting
b. Power III
c. Computer-assisted telephone interviewing
d. 180SearchAssistant

Chapter 11. Attitude Measurement

1. _____ refer to a collection of facts usually collected as the result of experience, observation or experiment or a set of premises. This may consist of numbers, words particularly as measurements or observations of a set of variables. _____ are often viewed as a lowest level of abstraction from which information and knowledge are derived.
   a. Pearson product-moment correlation coefficient
   b. DATA
   c. Sample size
   d. Mean

2. Cognition is the scientific term for 'the process of thought.' Its usage varies in different ways in accord with different disciplines: For example, in psychology and _____ science it refers to an information processing view of an individual's psychological functions. Other interpretations of the meaning of cognition link it to the development of concepts; individual minds, groups, organizations, and even larger coalitions of entities, can be modelled as 'societies' (Society of Mind), which cooperate to form concepts.

   The autonomous elements of each 'society' would have the opportunity to demonstrate emergent behavior in the face of some crisis or opportunity.

   a. Power III
   b. 6-3-5 Brainwriting
   c. 180SearchAssistant
   d. Cognitive

3. The '_____' is an expression which typically refers to the theory of scale types developed by the Harvard psychologist Stanley Smith Stevens In this article Stevens claimed that all measurement in science was conducted using four different types of numerical scales which he called 'nominal', 'ordinal', 'interval' and 'ratio'.
   a. 180SearchAssistant
   b. Power III
   c. Levels of measurement
   d. 6-3-5 Brainwriting

4. In grammar, the _____ is the form of an adjective or adverb which denotes the degree or grade by which a person, thing and is used in this context with a subordinating conjunction, such as than, as...as, etc.

   The structure of a _____ in English consists normally of the positive form of the adjective or adverb, plus the suffix -er e.g. 'he is taller than his father is', or 'the village is less picturesque than the town nearby'.

   a. 6-3-5 Brainwriting
   b. Power III
   c. Comparative
   d. 180SearchAssistant

5. A _____ is a collection of symbols, experiences and associations connected with a product, a service, a person or any other artifact or entity.

   _____s have become increasingly important components of culture and the economy, now being described as 'cultural accessories and personal philosophies'.

   Some people distinguish the psychological aspect of a _____ from the experiential aspect.

   a. Brand equity
   b. Brandable software
   c. Store brand
   d. Brand

Chapter 11. Attitude Measurement

6. _____ refers to the marketing effects or outcomes that accrue to a product with its brand name compared with those that would accrue if the same product did not have the brand name . And, at the root of these marketing effects is consumers' knowledge. In other words, consumers' knowledge about a brand makes manufacturers/advertisers respond differently or adopt appropriately adapt measures for the marketing of the brand .
   a. Brand image
   b. Brand aversion
   c. Product extension
   d. Brand equity

7. A _____ is a psychometric scale commonly used in questionnaires, and is the most widely used scale in survey research. When responding to a Likert questionnaire item, respondents specify their level of agreement to a statement. The scale is named after its inventor, psychologist Rensis Likert.
   a. Likert scale
   b. Factor analysis
   c. Power III
   d. Semantic differential

8. _____ is a marketing concept that refers to a consumer knowing of a brand's existence; at aggregate (brand) level it refers to the proportion of consumers who know of the brand.

   _____ can be measured by showing a consumer the brand and asking whether or not they knew of it beforehand. However, in common market research practice a variety of recognition and recall measures of _____ are employed all of which test the brand name's association to a product category cue, this came about because most market research in the 20th Century was conducted by post or telephone, actually showing the brand to consumers usually required more expensive face-to-face interviews (until web-based interviews became possible.)

   a. Fitting Group
   b. Brand orientation
   c. Brand equity
   d. Brand awareness

9. _____ is a parameter used in sociology, psychology, and other psychometric or behavioral sciences. _____ is demonstrated where a test correlates well with a measure that has previously been validated. The two measures may be for the same construct, or for different, but presumably related, constructs.
   a. Concurrent validity
   b. Discriminant validity
   c. Construct validity
   d. Criterion validity

10. In social science and psychometrics, _____ refers to whether a scale measures or correlates with a theorized psychological construct (such as 'fluid intelligence'.) It is related to the theoretical ideas behind the personality trait under consideration; a non-existent concept in the physical sense may be suggested as a method of organising how personality can be viewed. The unobservable idea of a unidimensional easier-to-harder dimension must be 'constructed' in the words of human language and graphics.
    a. Discriminant validity
    b. Construct validity
    c. Predictive validity
    d. Criterion validity

11. In the absence of a more specific context, convergence denotes the approach toward a definite value, as time goes on; or to a definite point, a common view or opinion, or toward a fixed or equilibrium state. _____ is the adjectival form, and also a noun meaning an iterative approximation.

In mathematics, convergence describes limiting behaviour, particularly of an infinite sequence or series, toward some limit.

a. Convergent
b. Strict liability
c. Good things come to those who wait
d. Geo

12. _____ is the degree to which an operation is similar to (converges on) other operations that it theoretically should also be similar to. For instance, to show the _____ of a test of mathematics skills, the scores on the test can be correlated with scores on other tests that are also designed to measure basic mathematics ability. High correlations between the test scores would be evidence of a _____.
a. Content validity
b. Convergent validity
c. Discriminant validity
d. Criterion validity

13. In psychometrics, _____ is a measure of how well one variable or set of variables predicts an outcome based on information from other variables, and will be achieved if a set of measures from a personality test relate to a behavioral criterion that psychologists agree on. A typical way to achieve this is in relation to the extent to which a score on a personality test can predict future performance or behaviour. Another way involves correlating test scores with another established test that also measures the same personality characteristic.
a. Construct validity
b. Convergent validity
c. Predictive validity
d. Criterion validity

14. In algebra, the _____ of a polynomial with real or complex coefficients is a certain expression in the coefficients of the polynomial which is equal to zero if and only if the polynomial has a multiple root (i.e. a root with multiplicity greater than one) in the complex numbers. For example, the _____ of the quadratic polynomial

$$ax^2 + bx + c \text{ is } b^2 - 4ac.$$

The _____ of the cubic polynomial

$$ax^3 + bx^2 + cx + d \text{ is } b^2c^2 - 4ac^3 - 4b^3d - 27a^2d^2 + 18abcd.$$

a. Discriminant
b. Consumption Map
c. Lifestyle center
d. Flighting

15. _____ describes the degree to which the operationalization is not similar to (diverges from) other operationalizations that it theoretically should not be similar to.

Campbell and Fiske (1959) introduced the concept of _____ within their discussion on evaluating test validity. They stressed the importance of using both discriminant and convergent validation techniques when assessing new tests.

a. Criterion validity
b. Convergent validity
c. Predictive validity
d. Discriminant validity

16. _____ is a property of a test intended to measure something. The test is said to have _____ if it 'looks like' it is going to measure what it is supposed to measure. For instance, if you prepare a test to measure whether students can perform multiplication, and the people you show it to all agree that it looks like a good test of multiplication ability, you have shown the _____ of your test.

a. Selective distortion
b. Power III
c. 180SearchAssistant
d. Face validity

17. A _____ is a statement or claim that a particular event will occur in the future in more certain terms than a forecast. The etymology of this word is Latin . In regards to predicting the future Howard H. Stevenson Says, ' _____ is at least two things: Important and hard.' Important, because we have to act, and hard because we have to realize the future we want, and what is the best way to get there.

a. 180SearchAssistant
b. 6-3-5 Brainwriting
c. Power III
d. Prediction

18. In psychometrics, _____ is the extent to which a score on a scale or test predicts scores on some criterion measure.

For example, the validity of a cognitive test for job performance is the correlation between test scores and, for example, supervisor performance ratings. Such a cognitive test would have _____ if the observed correlation were statistically significant.

a. Convergent validity
b. Predictive validity
c. Criterion validity
d. Discriminant validity

19. _____ is defined by the American _____ Association as the activity, set of institutions, and processes for creating, communicating, delivering, and exchanging offerings that have value for customers, clients, partners, and society at large. The term developed from the original meaning which referred literally to going to market, as in shopping, or going to a market to sell goods or services.

_____ practice tends to be seen as a creative industry, which includes advertising, distribution and selling.

a. Marketing myopia
b. Customer acquisition management
c. Product naming
d. Marketing

20. Consumer market research is a form of applied sociology that concentrates on understanding the behaviours, whims and preferences, of consumers in a market-based economy, and aims to understand the effects and comparative success of marketing campaigns. The field of consumer _____ as a statistical science was pioneered by Arthur Nielsen with the founding of the ACNielsen Company in 1923 .

Thus _____ is the systematic and objective identification, collection, analysis, and dissemination of information for the purpose of assisting management in decision making related to the identification and solution of problems and opportunities in marketing.

a. Focus group
b. Marketing research process
c. Logit analysis
d. Marketing research

Chapter 12. Designing the Questionnaire

1. A _____ is a research instrument consisting of a series of questions and other prompts for the purpose of gathering information from respondents. Although they are often designed for statistical analysis of the responses, this is not always the case. The _____ was invented by Sir Francis Galton.
   a. Mystery shoppers
   b. Mystery shopping
   c. Market research
   d. Questionnaire

2. _____ in organizations and public policy is both the organizational process of creating and maintaining a plan; and the psychological process of thinking about the activities required to create a desired goal on some scale. As such, it is a fundamental property of intelligent behavior. This thought process is essential to the creation and refinement of a plan, or integration of it with other plans, that is, it combines forecasting of developments with the preparation of scenarios of how to react to them.
   a. 180SearchAssistant
   b. 6-3-5 Brainwriting
   c. Power III
   d. Planning

3. _____ is a compliance tactic that involves getting a person to agree to a large request by first setting them up by having that person agree to a modest request.

   In an early study, a team of psychologists telephoned housewives in California and asked if the women would answer a few questions about the household products they used. Three days later, the psychologists called again.

   a. 180SearchAssistant
   b. 6-3-5 Brainwriting
   c. Power III
   d. Foot-in-the-door technique

4. _____ is a standard point of view or personal prejudice. especially when the tendency interferes with the ability to be impartial, unprejudiced, or objective. The term _____ed is used to describe an action, judgment, or other outcome influenced by a prejudged perspective.
   a. Bias
   b. 6-3-5 Brainwriting
   c. Power III
   d. 180SearchAssistant

5. _____ is a fee paid on borrowed assets. It is the price paid for the use of borrowed money , or, money earned by deposited funds . Assets that are sometimes lent with _____ include money, shares, consumer goods through hire purchase, major assets such as aircraft, and even entire factories in finance lease arrangements.
   a. ADTECH
   b. ACNielsen
   c. AMAX
   d. Interest

Chapter 13. Experimentation

1. _____ denotes a necessary relationship between one event and another event (called effect) which is the direct consequence of the first.

While this informal understanding suffices in everyday use, the philosophical analysis of how best to characterize _____ extends over millennia. In the western philosophical tradition explicit discussion stretches back at least as far as Aristotle, and the topic remains a staple in contemporary philosophy journals.

- a. Causality
- b. 180SearchAssistant
- c. Power III
- d. 6-3-5 Brainwriting

2. _____ is a statistical method used to describe variability among observed variables in terms of fewer unobserved variables called factors. The observed variables are modeled as linear combinations of the factors, plus 'error' terms. The information gained about the interdependencies can be used later to reduce the set of variables in a dataset.
- a. Factor analysis
- b. Semantic differential
- c. Likert scale
- d. Power III

3. _____,, is a common tool in the retail industry to create the look of a perfectly stocked store by pulling all of the products on a display or shelf to the front, as well as downstacking all the canned and stacked items. It is also done to keep the store appearing neat and organized.

The workers who face commonly have jobs doing other things in the store such as customer service, stocking shelves, daytime cleaning, bagging and carryouts, etc.

- a. Facing
- b. Customer Integrated System
- c. Foviance
- d. Customer Experience Analytics

4. Though criteria for causality in statistical studies have been researched intensely, Pearl has shown that _____ cannot be defined in terms of statistical notions alone; some causal assumptions are necessary. In a 1965 paper, Austin Bradford Hill proposed a set of causal criteria.. Many working epidemiologists take these as a good place to start when considering confounding and causation.
- a. T-test
- b. Linear regression
- c. Survey research
- d. Confounding variables

5. _____ are a vital part of the scientific method, since they can eliminate or minimise unintended influences such as researcher bias, environmental changes and biological variation. Controlled experiments are used to investigate the effect of a variable on a particular system. In a controlled one set of samples have been (or is believed to be) modified and the other set of samples are either expected to show no change (negative control) or expected to show a definite change (positive control.)
- a. Pearson's chi-square
- b. Clutter
- c. Little value placed on potential benefits
- d. Scientific controls

6. In economics, _____ is the desire to own something and the ability to pay for it. The term _____ signifies the ability or the willingness to buy a particular commodity at a given point of time .

Chapter 13. Experimentation

a. Demand
b. Market system
c. Market dominance
d. Discretionary spending

7. In research, and particularly psychology, _____ refers to an experimental artifact where participants form an interpretation of the experiment's purpose and unconsciously change their behavior accordingly. Pioneering research was conducted on _____ by Martin Orne. Typically, they are considered a confounding variable, exerting an effect on behavior other than that intended by the experimenter.

a. Power III
b. 180SearchAssistant
c. 6-3-5 Brainwriting
d. Demand characteristics

8. The terms '_____' and 'independent variable' are used in similar but subtly different ways in mathematics and statistics as part of the standard terminology in those subjects. They are used to distinguish between two types of quantities being considered, separating them into those available at the start of a process and those being created by it, where the latter (_____s) are dependent on the former (independent variables.)

In traditional calculus, a function is defined as a relation between two terms called variables because their values vary.

a. Dependent variable
b. 180SearchAssistant
c. Field experiment
d. Power III

9. _____ are variables other than the independent variable that may bear any effect on the behavior of the subject being studied.

_____ are often classified into three main types:

1. Subject variables, which are the characteristics of the individuals being studied that might affect their actions. These variables include age, gender, health status, mood, background, etc.
2. Experimental variables are characteristics of the persons conducting the experiment which might influence how a person behaves. Gender, the presence of racial discrimination, language, or other factors may qualify as such variables.
3. Situational variables are features of the environment in which the study or research was conducted, which have a bearing on the outcome of the experiment in a negative way. Included are the air temperature, level of activity, lighting, and the time of day.

There are two strategies of controlling _____. Either a potentially influential variable is kept the same for all subjects in the research, or they balance the variables in a group.

Take for example an experiment, in which a salesperson sells clothing on a door-to-door basis.

a. Extraneous variables
b. AMAX
c. ACNielsen
d. ADTECH

10. The _____ is a form of reactivity, The term was coined in 1955 by Henry A. Landsberger when analyzing older experiments from 1924-1932 at the Hawthorne Works (outside Chicago.) Landsberger defined the _____ as:

Chapter 13. Experimentation

- a short-term improvement caused by observing worker performance.

Earlier researchers had concluded the short-term improvement was caused by teamwork when workers saw themselves as part of a study group or team. Others have broadened the definition to mean that people's behavior and performance change following any new or increased attention. Hence, the term _____ no longer has a specific definition.

a. Power III
b. 6-3-5 Brainwriting
c. 180SearchAssistant
d. Hawthorne effect

11. In the mathematical discipline of graph theory a _____ or edge-independent set in a graph is a set of edges without common vertices. It may also be an entire graph consisting of edges without common vertices.

Given a graph G = (V,E), a _____ M in G is a set of pairwise non-adjacent edges; that is, no two edges share a common vertex.

a. 6-3-5 Brainwriting
b. 180SearchAssistant
c. Power III
d. Matching

12. _____ is the process of making something random; this means:

- Generating a random permutation of a sequence (such as when shuffling cards.)
- Selecting a random sample of a population (important in statistical sampling.)
- Generating random numbers: see Random number generation.
- Transforming a data stream using a scrambler in telecommunications.

_____ is used extensively in the field of gambling (or generally being random.) Imperfect _____ may allow a skilled gambler to have an advantage, so much research has been devoted to effective _____. A classic example of _____ is shuffling playing cards.

_____ is a core principle in the statistical theory of design of experiments.

a. Randomization
b. Standard deviation
c. Sample size
d. Statistics

13. _____ is a distortion of evidence or data that arises from the way that the data are collected. It is sometimes referred to as the selection effect. The term _____ most often refers to the distortion of a statistical analysis, due to the method of collecting samples.

a. Power III
b. Systematic sampling
c. 180SearchAssistant
d. Selection bias

14. _____ is a standard point of view or personal prejudice. especially when the tendency interferes with the ability to be impartial, unprejudiced, or objective. The term _____ed is used to describe an action, judgment, or other outcome influenced by a prejudged perspective.

Chapter 13. Experimentation

a. 6-3-5 Brainwriting
c. Bias
b. 180SearchAssistant
d. Power III

15. _____s are used in open sentences. For instance, in the formula x + 1 = 5, x is a _____ which represents an 'unknown' number. _____s are often represented by letters of the Roman alphabet, or those of other alphabets, such as Greek, and use other special symbols.
a. Quantitative
c. Book of business
b. Variable
d. Personalization

16. _____ is the validity of (causal) inferences in scientific studies, usually based on experiments as experimental validity .

Inferences are said to possess _____ if a causal relation between two variables is properly demonstrated . A causal inference may be based on a relation when three criteria are satisfied:

1. the 'cause' precedes the 'effect' in time (temporal precedence),
2. the 'cause' and the 'effect' are related (covariation), and
3. there are no plausible alternative explanations for the observed covariation (nonspuriousness) .

In scientific experimental settings, researchers often manipulate a variable (the independent variable) to see what effect it has on a second variable (the dependent variable) For example, a researcher might, for different experimental groups, manipulate the dosage of a particular drug between groups to see what effect it has on health. In this example, the researcher wants to make a causal inference, namely, that different doses of the drug may be held responsible for observed changes or differences.

a. ACNielsen
c. AMAX
b. ADTECH
d. Internal validity

17. In the design of experiments, _____ are for studying the effects of one primary factor without the need to take other nuisance factors into account The experiment compares the values of a response variable based on the different levels of that primary factor.
a. Comprehensive,
c. Geo
b. Just-In-Case
d. Completely randomized designs

18. In statistics, an _____ is a term in a statistical model added when the effect of two or more variables is not simply additive. Such a term reflects that the effect of one variable depends on the values of one or more other variables.

Thus, for a response Y and two variables x_1 and x_2 an additive model would be:

$$Y = ax_1 + bx_2 + \text{error}$$

In contrast to this,

$$Y = ax_1 + bx_2 + c(x_1 \times x_2) + \text{error},$$

is an example of a model with an _____ between variables x_1 and x_2 ('error' refers to the random variable whose value by which y differs from the expected value of y.)

a. AMAX
b. ACNielsen
c. Interaction
d. ADTECH

19. In economics, an externality or spillover of an economic transaction is an impact on a party that is not directly involved in the transaction. In such a case, prices do not reflect the full costs or benefits in production or consumption of a product or service. A positive impact is called an _____ benefit, while a negative impact is called an _____ cost.

a. External
b. AMAX
c. ACNielsen
d. ADTECH

20. A _____ applies the scientific method to experimentally examine an intervention in the real world (or as many experimental economists like to say, naturally-occurring environments) rather than in the laboratory. _____s, like lab experiments, generally randomize subjects (or other sampling units) into treatment and control groups and compare outcomes between these groups. Clinical trials of pharmaceuticals are one example of _____s.

a. Power III
b. Response variable
c. 180SearchAssistant
d. Field experiment

21. A supply chain is the system of organizations, people, technology, activities, information and resources involved in moving a product or service from _____ to customer. Supply chain activities transform natural resources, raw materials and components into a finished product that is delivered to the end customer. In sophisticated supply chain systems, used products may re-enter the supply chain at any point where residual value is recyclable.

a. Rebate
b. Supplier
c. Product line extension
d. Bringin' Home the Oil

22. _____ is the validity of generalized (causal) inferences in scientific studies, usually based on experiments as experimental validity.

Inferences about cause-effect relationships based on a specific scientific study are said to possess _____ if they may be generalized from the unique and idiosyncratic settings, procedures and participants to other populations and conditions Causal inferences said to possess high degrees of _____ can reasonably be expected to apply (a) to the target population of the study (i.e. from which the sample was drawn) (also referred to as population validity), and (b) to the universe of other populations (e.g. across time and space.)

The most common loss of _____ comes from the fact that experiments using human participants often employ small samples obtained from a single geographic location or with idiosyncratic features (e.g. volunteers.)

Chapter 13. Experimentation

a. External validity
c. AMAX
b. ACNielsen
d. ADTECH

23. _____ generally refers to a list of all planned expenses and revenues. It is a plan for saving and spending. A _____ is an important concept in microeconomics, which uses a _____ line to illustrate the trade-offs between two or more goods.

a. Power III
c. 180SearchAssistant
b. 6-3-5 Brainwriting
d. Budget

24. In economics, business, retail, and accounting, a _____ is the value of money that has been used up to produce something, and hence is not available for use anymore. In economics, a _____ is an alternative that is given up as a result of a decision. In business, the _____ may be one of acquisition, in which case the amount of money expended to acquire it is counted as _____.

a. Fixed costs
c. Transaction cost
b. Cost
d. Variable cost

25. Competitiveness is a comparative concept of the ability and performance of a firm, sub-sector or country to sell and supply goods and/or services in a given market. Although widely used in economics and business management, the usefulness of the concept, particularly in the context of national competitiveness, is vigorously disputed by economists, such as Paul Krugman .

The term may also be applied to markets, where it is used to refer to the extent to which the market structure may be regarded as perfectly _____.

a. Customs union
c. Free trade zone
b. Geographical pricing
d. Competitive

26. _____ is, in very basic words, a position a firm occupies against its competitors.

According to Michael Porter, the three methods for creating a sustainable _____ are through:

1. Cost leadership - Cost advantage occurs when a firm delivers the same services as its competitors but at a lower cost;

2.

a. 180SearchAssistant
c. 6-3-5 Brainwriting
b. Power III
d. Competitive advantage

27. _____ is the presence of a minor constituent in another chemical or mixture, often at the trace level. In chemistry, the term usually describes a single chemical, but in specialized fields the term can also mean chemical mixtures, even up to the level of cellular materials.

All chemicals contain some level of _____.

Chapter 13. Experimentation

a. Contamination
b. 180SearchAssistant
c. 6-3-5 Brainwriting
d. Power III

28. _____ is the realization of an application idea, model, design, specification, standard, algorithm an _____ is a realization of a technical specification or algorithm as a program, software component, or other computer system. Many _____s may exist for a given specification or standard.

a. ADTECH
b. AMAX
c. ACNielsen
d. Implementation

29. _____ is either an activity of a living being (such as a human), consisting of receiving knowledge of the outside world through the senses, or the recording of data using scientific instruments. The term may also refer to any datum collected during this activity.

The scientific method requires _____s of nature to formulate and test hypotheses.

a. Observation
b. ACNielsen
c. AMAX
d. ADTECH

30. _____ is the imitation of some real thing, state of affairs, or process. The act of simulating something generally entails representing certain key characteristics or behaviors of a selected physical or abstract system.

_____ is used in many contexts, including the modeling of natural systems or human systems in order to gain insight into their functioning.

a. 6-3-5 Brainwriting
b. Power III
c. 180SearchAssistant
d. Simulation

31. _____ is defined by the American _____ Association as the activity, set of institutions, and processes for creating, communicating, delivering, and exchanging offerings that have value for customers, clients, partners, and society at large. The term developed from the original meaning which referred literally to going to market, as in shopping, or going to a market to sell goods or services.

_____ practice tends to be seen as a creative industry, which includes advertising, distribution and selling.

a. Customer acquisition management
b. Marketing myopia
c. Marketing
d. Product naming

32. A _____, in the field of business and marketing, is a geographic region or demographic group used to gauge the viability of a product or service in the mass market prior to a wide scale roll-out. The criteria used to judge the acceptability of a _____ region or group include:

1. a population that is demographically similar to the proposed target market; and
2. relative isolation from densely populated media markets so that advertising to the test audience can be efficient and economical.

Chapter 13. Experimentation

The _____ ideally aims to duplicate 'everything' - promotion and distribution as well as `product' - on a smaller scale. The technique replicates, typically in one area, what is planned to occur in a national launch; and the results are very carefully monitored, so that they can be extrapolated to projected national results. The `area' may be any one of the following:

- Television area
- Test town
- Residential neighborhood
- Test site

A number of decisions have to be taken about any _____:

- Which _____?
- What is to be tested?
- How long a test?
- What are the success criteria?

The simple go or no-go decision, together with the related reduction of risk, is normally the main justification for the expense of _____s. At the same time, however, such _____s can be used to test specific elements of a new product's marketing mix; possibly the version of the product itself, the promotional message and media spend, the distribution channels and the price.

a. Power III
b. Test market
c. Preadolescence
d. 180SearchAssistant

Chapter 14. Sampling Fundamentals

1. The _____ of a statistical sample is the number of observations that constitute it. It is typically denoted n, a positive integer (natural number.)

Typically, all else being equal, a larger _____ leads to increased precision in estimates of various properties of the population.

    a. Data
    b. Frequency distribution
    c. Heteroskedastic
    d. Sample size

2. _____ is anything that is intended to save time, energy or frustration. A _____ store at a petrol station, for example, sells items that have nothing to do with gasoline/petrol, but it saves the consumer from having to go to a grocery store. '_____' is a very relative term and its meaning tends to change over time.
    a. Marketing buzz
    b. Demographic profile
    c. MaxDiff
    d. Convenience

3. _____ is a type of nonprobability sampling which involves the sample being drawn from that part of the population which is close to hand. That is, a sample population selected because it is readily available and convenient. The researcher using such a sample cannot scientifically make generalizations about the total population from this sample because it would not be representative enough.
    a. AMAX
    b. ADTECH
    c. ACNielsen
    d. Accidental sampling

4. 'Speaking generally, properties are those physical quantities which directly describe the physical attributes of the system; _____s are those combinations of the properties which suffice to determine the response of the system. Properties can have all sorts of dimensions, depending upon the system being considered; _____s are dimensionless, or have the dimension of time or its reciprocal.'

The term can also be used in engineering contexts, however, as it is typically used in the physical sciences.

When the terms formal _____ and actual _____ are used, they generally correspond with the definitions used in computer science.

    a. 180SearchAssistant
    b. Power III
    c. 6-3-5 Brainwriting
    d. Parameter

5. _____ is that part of statistical practice concerned with the selection of individual observations intended to yield some knowledge about a population of concern, especially for the purposes of statistical inference. Each observation measures one or more properties (weight, location, etc.) of an observable entity enumerated to distinguish objects or individuals.
    a. Sports Marketing Group
    b. AStore
    c. Richard Buckminster 'Bucky' Fuller
    d. Sampling

6. _____ is a mathematical science pertaining to the collection, analysis, interpretation or explanation, and presentation of data. It also provides tools for prediction and forecasting based on data. It is applicable to a wide variety of academic disciplines, from the natural and social sciences to the humanities, government and business.

a. Null hypothesis
c. Median
b. Statistics
d. Type I error

7. In statistics, _____ or estimation error is the error caused by observing a sample instead of the whole population.

An estimate of a quantity of interest, such as an average or percentage, will generally be subject to sample-to-sample variation. These variations in the possible sample values of a statistic can theoretically be expressed as _____s, although in practice the exact _____ is typically unknown.

a. Sampling Error
c. Two-tailed test
b. Varimax rotation
d. Power III

8. In statistics, _____ has two related meanings:

- the arithmetic _____
- the expected value of a random variable, which is also called the population _____.

It is sometimes stated that the '_____' _____s average. This is incorrect if '_____' is taken in the specific sense of 'arithmetic _____' as there are different types of averages: the _____, median, and mode. For instance, average house prices almost always use the median value for the average. These three types of averages are all measures of locations.

a. Heteroskedastic
c. Standard normal distribution
b. Mean
d. Confidence interval

9. Sampling is the use of a subset of the population to represent the whole population. Probability sampling, or random sampling, is a sampling technique in which the probability of getting any particular sample may be calculated. _____ does not meet this criterion and should be used with caution.

a. Power III
c. Snowball sampling
b. Quota sampling
d. Nonprobability sampling

10. _____ is a way of expressing knowledge or belief that an event will occur or has occurred. In mathematics the concept has been given an exact meaning in _____ theory, that is used extensively in such areas of study as mathematics, statistics, finance, gambling, science, and philosophy to draw conclusions about the likelihood of potential events and the underlying mechanics of complex systems.

a. Heteroskedastic
c. Probability
b. Data
d. Linear regression

11. In statistics, a simple random sample is a subset of individuals (a sample) chosen from a larger set (a population.) Each individual is chosen randomly and entirely by chance, such that each individual has the same probability of being chosen at any stage during the sampling process, and each subset of k individuals has the same probability of being chosen for the sample as any other subset of k individuals (.) This process and technique is known as _____, and should not be confused with Random Sampling.

a. Focus group
c. Logit analysis
b. Market analysis
d. Simple random sampling

Chapter 14. Sampling Fundamentals

12. _____ generally refers to a list of all planned expenses and revenues. It is a plan for saving and spending. A _____ is an important concept in microeconomics, which uses a _____ line to illustrate the trade-offs between two or more goods.

   a. Budget
   b. Power III
   c. 6-3-5 Brainwriting
   d. 180SearchAssistant

13. In economics, business, retail, and accounting, a _____ is the value of money that has been used up to produce something, and hence is not available for use anymore. In economics, a _____ is an alternative that is given up as a result of a decision. In business, the _____ may be one of acquisition, in which case the amount of money expended to acquire it is counted as _____.

   a. Fixed costs
   b. Variable cost
   c. Transaction cost
   d. Cost

14. In statistics, _____ is a method of sampling from a population.

When sub-populations vary considerably, it is advantageous to sample each subpopulation (stratum) independently. Stratification is the process of grouping members of the population into relatively homogeneous subgroups before sampling.

   a. Data
   b. Coefficient of variation
   c. T-test
   d. Stratified sampling

15. Competitiveness is a comparative concept of the ability and performance of a firm, sub-sector or country to sell and supply goods and/or services in a given market. Although widely used in economics and business management, the usefulness of the concept, particularly in the context of national competitiveness, is vigorously disputed by economists, such as Paul Krugman .

The term may also be applied to markets, where it is used to refer to the extent to which the market structure may be regarded as perfectly _____.

   a. Competitive
   b. Customs union
   c. Free trade zone
   d. Geographical pricing

16. _____ is, in very basic words, a position a firm occupies against its competitors.

According to Michael Porter, the three methods for creating a sustainable _____ are through:

1. Cost leadership - Cost advantage occurs when a firm delivers the same services as its competitors but at a lower cost;

2.

   a. Power III
   b. Competitive advantage
   c. 6-3-5 Brainwriting
   d. 180SearchAssistant

Chapter 14. Sampling Fundamentals

17. In mathematics, the _____ or Euclidean metric is the 'ordinary' distance between two points that one would measure with a ruler, which can be proven by repeated application of the Pythagorean theorem. By using this formula as distance, Euclidean space becomes a metric space (even a Hilbert space.) The associated norm is called the Euclidean norm.
    a. ADTECH
    b. ACNielsen
    c. AMAX
    d. Euclidean distance

18. _____ is a sampling technique used when 'natural' groupings are evident in a statistical population. It is often used in marketing research. In this technique, the total population is divided into these groups (or clusters) and a sample of the groups is selected.
    a. Quota sampling
    b. Power III
    c. Cluster sampling
    d. Snowball sampling

19. _____ is a statistical method involving the selection of elements from an ordered sampling frame. The most common form of _____ is an equal-probability method, in which every k^{th} element in the frame is selected, where k, the sampling interval (sometimes known as the 'skip'), is calculated as:

    sample size (n) = population size (N) /k

    Using this procedure each element in the population has a known and equal probability of selection. This makes _____ functionally similar to simple random sampling.

    a. Selection bias
    b. 180SearchAssistant
    c. Systematic sampling
    d. Power III

20. In social science research, _____ is a technique for developing a research sample where existing study subjects recruit future subjects from among their acquaintances. Thus the sample group appears to grow like a rolling snowball. As the sample builds up, enough data is gathered to be useful for research.
    a. Nonprobability sampling
    b. Quota sampling
    c. Power III
    d. Snowball sampling

21. In _____, the population is first segmented into mutually exclusive sub-groups, just as in stratified sampling. Then judgment is used to select the subjects or units from each segment based on a specified proportion. For example, an interviewer may be told to sample 200 females and 300 males between the age of 45 and 60.
    a. Snowball sampling
    b. Power III
    c. Nonprobability sampling
    d. Quota sampling

22. _____ is a standard point of view or personal prejudice. especially when the tendency interferes with the ability to be impartial, unprejudiced, or objective. The term _____ed is used to describe an action, judgment, or other outcome influenced by a prejudged perspective.
    a. 180SearchAssistant
    b. Power III
    c. Bias
    d. 6-3-5 Brainwriting

Chapter 14. Sampling Fundamentals

23. A number of different _____s are indicated below.

- Randomized controlled trial
    - Double-blind randomized trial
    - Single-blind randomized trial
    - Non-blind trial
- Nonrandomized trial (quasi-experiment)
    - Interrupted time series design (measures on a sample or a series of samples from the same population are obtained several times before and after a manipulated event or a naturally occurring event) - considered a type of quasi-experiment

- Cohort study
    - Prospective cohort
    - Retrospective cohort
    - Time series study
- Case-control study
    - Nested case-control study
- Cross-sectional study
    - Community survey (a type of cross-sectional study)

When choosing a _____, many factors must be taken into account. Different types of studies are subject to different types of bias. For example, recall bias is likely to occur in cross-sectional or case-control studies where subjects are asked to recall exposure to risk factors.

a. Power III
c. 180SearchAssistant
b. Longitudinal studies
d. Study design

24. _____ is the examining of goods or services from retailers with the intent to purchase at that time. _____ is an activity of selection and/or purchase. In some contexts it is considered a leisure activity as well as an economic one.

a. Discount store
c. Khodebshchik
b. Shopping
d. Hawkers

Chapter 15. Sample Size and Statistical Theory

1. The _____ of a statistical sample is the number of observations that constitute it. It is typically denoted n, a positive integer (natural number.)

Typically, all else being equal, a larger _____ leads to increased precision in estimates of various properties of the population.

a. Data
c. Heteroskedastic
b. Sample size
d. Frequency distribution

2. _____ is that part of statistical practice concerned with the selection of individual observations intended to yield some knowledge about a population of concern, especially for the purposes of statistical inference. Each observation measures one or more properties (weight, location, etc.) of an observable entity enumerated to distinguish objects or individuals.

a. Sports Marketing Group
c. AStore
b. Richard Buckminster 'Bucky' Fuller
d. Sampling

3. _____ generally refers to a list of all planned expenses and revenues. It is a plan for saving and spending. A _____ is an important concept in microeconomics, which uses a _____ line to illustrate the trade-offs between two or more goods.

a. Power III
c. Budget
b. 6-3-5 Brainwriting
d. 180SearchAssistant

4. In economics, business, retail, and accounting, a _____ is the value of money that has been used up to produce something, and hence is not available for use anymore. In economics, a _____ is an alternative that is given up as a result of a decision. In business, the _____ may be one of acquisition, in which case the amount of money expended to acquire it is counted as _____.

a. Cost
c. Fixed costs
b. Variable cost
d. Transaction cost

5. _____ is a form of communication that typically attempts to persuade potential customers to purchase or to consume more of a particular brand of product or service. 'While now central to the contemporary global economy and the reproduction of global production networks, it is only quite recently that _____ has been more than a marginal influence on patterns of sales and production. The formation of modern _____ was intimately bound up with the emergence of new forms of monopoly capitalism around the end of the 19th and beginning of the 20th century as one element in corporate strategies to create, organize and where possible control markets, especially for mass produced consumer goods.

a. AMAX
c. ACNielsen
b. Advertising
d. ADTECH

6. Competitiveness is a comparative concept of the ability and performance of a firm, sub-sector or country to sell and supply goods and/or services in a given market. Although widely used in economics and business management, the usefulness of the concept, particularly in the context of national competitiveness, is vigorously disputed by economists, such as Paul Krugman .

The term may also be applied to markets, where it is used to refer to the extent to which the market structure may be regarded as perfectly _____.

Chapter 15. Sample Size and Statistical Theory

a. Free trade zone
b. Customs union
c. Geographical pricing
d. Competitive

7. _____ is, in very basic words, a position a firm occupies against its competitors.

According to Michael Porter, the three methods for creating a sustainable _____ are through:

1. Cost leadership - Cost advantage occurs when a firm delivers the same services as its competitors but at a lower cost;

2.

a. 180SearchAssistant
b. Power III
c. 6-3-5 Brainwriting
d. Competitive advantage

8. In statistics, _____ has two related meanings:

- the arithmetic _____
- the expected value of a random variable, which is also called the population _____.

It is sometimes stated that the '_____' _____s average. This is incorrect if '_____' is taken in the specific sense of 'arithmetic _____' as there are different types of averages: the _____, median, and mode. For instance, average house prices almost always use the median value for the average. These three types of averages are all measures of locations.

a. Mean
b. Standard normal distribution
c. Confidence interval
d. Heteroskedastic

9. 'Speaking generally, properties are those physical quantities which directly describe the physical attributes of the system; _____s are those combinations of the properties which suffice to determine the response of the system. Properties can have all sorts of dimensions, depending upon the system being considered; _____s are dimensionless, or have the dimension of time or its reciprocal.'

The term can also be used in engineering contexts, however, as it is typically used in the physical sciences.

When the terms formal _____ and actual _____ are used, they generally correspond with the definitions used in computer science.

a. 6-3-5 Brainwriting
b. Power III
c. 180SearchAssistant
d. Parameter

10. In statistics, _____ is a simple measure of the variability or dispersion of a data set. A low _____ indicates that the data points tend to be very close to the same value (the mean), while high _____ indicates that the data are 'spread out' over a large range of values.

Chapter 15. Sample Size and Statistical Theory

For example, the average height for adult men in the United States is about 70 inches, with a _____ of around 3 inches.

a. Z-test
b. Statistically significant
c. Standard deviation
d. Pearson product-moment correlation coefficient

11. In probability theory and statistics, the _____ of a random variable, probability distribution, or sample is a measure of statistical dispersion, averaging the squared distance of its possible values from the expected value (mean.) Whereas the mean is a way to describe the location of a distribution, the _____ is a way to capture its scale or degree of being spread out. The unit of _____ is the square of the unit of the original variable.

a. Standard deviation
b. Variance
c. Correlation
d. Sample size

12. In mathematics and statistics, the arithmetic mean (or simply the mean) of a list of numbers is the sum of all of the list divided by the number of items in the list. If the list is a statistical population, then the mean of that population is called a population mean. If the list is a statistical sample, we call the resulting statistic a _____.

a. Sample mean
b. Null hypothesis
c. Z-test
d. Coefficient of variation

13. In statistics, _____ is the use of sample data to calculate an interval of possible (or probable) values of an unknown population parameter, in contrast to point estimation, which is a single number. Neyman (1937) identified _____ as distinct from point estimation ('estimation by unique estimate'.) In doing so, he recognised that then-recent work quoting results in the form of an estimate plus-or-minus a standard deviation indicated that _____ was actually the problem statisticians really had in mind.

a. Interval estimation
b. ACNielsen
c. Arithmetic mean
d. Analysis of variance

14. In population genetics and population ecology, _____ is the number of individual organisms in a population.

The effective _____ (N_e) is defined as 'the number of breeding individuals in an idealized population that would show the same amount of dispersion of allele frequencies under random genetic drift or the same amount of inbreeding as the population under consideration.' N_e is usually less than N (the absolute _____) and this has important applications in conservation genetics.

Small _____ results in increased genetic drift.

a. 6-3-5 Brainwriting
b. Population size
c. Power III
d. 180SearchAssistant

15. In probability theory and statistics, the _____ is a normalized measure of dispersion of a probability distribution. It is defined as the ratio of the standard deviation σ to the mean μ:

$$c_v = \frac{\sigma}{\mu}$$

This is only defined for non-zero mean, and is most useful for variables that are always positive. It is also known as unitized risk.

a. Mean
b. Control chart
c. Coefficient of variation
d. Statistical hypothesis test

16. In statistics, _____ or estimation error is the error caused by observing a sample instead of the whole population.

An estimate of a quantity of interest, such as an average or percentage, will generally be subject to sample-to-sample variation. These variations in the possible sample values of a statistic can theoretically be expressed as _____s, although in practice the exact _____ is typically unknown.

a. Power III
b. Two-tailed test
c. Varimax rotation
d. Sampling error

17. In statistics, _____ is a method of sampling from a population.

When sub-populations vary considerably, it is advantageous to sample each subpopulation (stratum) independently. Stratification is the process of grouping members of the population into relatively homogeneous subgroups before sampling.

a. Coefficient of variation
b. Data
c. T-test
d. Stratified sampling

Chapter 16. Fundamentals of Data Analysis

1. _____ refer to a collection of facts usually collected as the result of experience, observation or experiment or a set of premises. This may consist of numbers, words particularly as measurements or observations of a set of variables. _____ are often viewed as a lowest level of abstraction from which information and knowledge are derived.
   a. Mean
   b. Sample size
   c. Pearson product-moment correlation coefficient
   d. Data

2. _____ is a process of gathering, modeling, and transforming data with the goal of highlighting useful information, suggesting conclusions, and supporting decision making. _____ has multiple facets and approaches, encompassing diverse techniques under a variety of names, in different business, science, and social science domains.

   Data mining is a particular _____ technique that focuses on modeling and knowledge discovery for predictive rather than purely descriptive purposes.

   a. Power III
   b. 180SearchAssistant
   c. Data analysis
   d. 6-3-5 Brainwriting

3. _____ is a mathematical science pertaining to the collection, analysis, interpretation or explanation, and presentation of data. It also provides tools for prediction and forecasting based on data. It is applicable to a wide variety of academic disciplines, from the natural and social sciences to the humanities, government and business.
   a. Type I error
   b. Median
   c. Null hypothesis
   d. Statistics

4. The process of _____ involves emphasising some aspects of a phenomenon, or of a set of data -- giving them 'more weight' in the final effect or result. It is analogous to the practice of adding extra weight to one side of a pair of scales to favour a buyer or seller.

   While _____ may be applied to a set of data, for example epidemiological data, it is more commonly applied to measurements of light, heat, sound, gamma radiation, in fact any stimulus that is spread over a spectrum of frequencies.

   a. 180SearchAssistant
   b. 6-3-5 Brainwriting
   c. Power III
   d. Weighting

5. _____s are used in open sentences. For instance, in the formula x + 1 = 5, x is a _____ which represents an 'unknown' number. _____s are often represented by letters of the Roman alphabet, or those of other alphabets, such as Greek, and use other special symbols.
   a. Variable
   b. Book of business
   c. Personalization
   d. Quantitative

6. In statistics, econometrics, epidemiology and related disciplines, the method of _____ is used to estimate causal relationships when controlled experiments are not feasible.

   Statistically, _____ methods allow consistent estimation when the explanatory variables (covariates) are correlated with the error terms. Such correlation may occur when the dependent variable causes at least one of the of covariates ('reverse' causation), when there are relevant explanatory variables which are omitted from the model, or when the covariates are subject to measurement error.

Chapter 16. Fundamentals of Data Analysis

a. ACNielsen
c. AMAX
b. ADTECH
d. Instrumental variables

7. A _____ is a plan of action designed to achieve a particular goal.

_____ is different from tactics. In military terms, tactics is concerned with the conduct of an engagement while _____ is concerned with how different engagements are linked.

a. Power III
c. 6-3-5 Brainwriting
b. 180SearchAssistant
d. Strategy

8. In statistics, a _____ is a tabulation of the values that one or more variables take in a sample.

Univariate _____s are often presented as lists, ordered by quantity, showing the number of times each value appears. For example, if 100 people rate a five-point Likert scale assessing their agreement with a statement on a scale on which 1 denotes strong agreement and 5 strong disagreement, the _____ of their responses might look like:

This simple tabulation has two drawbacks.

a. Confidence interval
c. Statistics
b. Survey research
d. Frequency distribution

9. _____ is one of the four elements of marketing mix. An organization or set of organizations (go-betweens) involved in the process of making a product or service available for use or consumption by a consumer or business user.

The other three parts of the marketing mix are product, pricing, and promotion.

a. Better Living Through Chemistry
c. Distribution
b. Japan Advertising Photographers' Association
d. Comparison-Shopping agent

10. _____ are used to describe the basic features of the data gathered from an experimental study in various ways. A _____ is distinguished from inductive statistics. They provide simple summaries about the sample and the measures.

a. P-Value
c. Pearson product-moment correlation coefficient
b. Frequency distribution
d. Descriptive statistics

11. In statistics, _____ has two related meanings:

- the arithmetic _____
- the expected value of a random variable, which is also called the population _____.

It is sometimes stated that the '_____' _____s average. This is incorrect if '_____' is taken in the specific sense of 'arithmetic _____' as there are different types of averages: the _____, median, and mode. For instance, average house prices almost always use the median value for the average. These three types of averages are all measures of locations.

a. Standard normal distribution
c. Confidence interval
b. Heteroskedastic
d. Mean

12. The '_____' is an expression which typically refers to the theory of scale types developed by the Harvard psychologist Stanley Smith Stevens In this article Stevens claimed that all measurement in science was conducted using four different types of numerical scales which he called 'nominal', 'ordinal', 'interval' and 'ratio'.

a. 180SearchAssistant
c. 6-3-5 Brainwriting
b. Power III
d. Levels of measurement

13. A number of different _____s are indicated below.

- Randomized controlled trial
    - Double-blind randomized trial
    - Single-blind randomized trial
    - Non-blind trial
- Nonrandomized trial (quasi-experiment)
    - Interrupted time series design (measures on a sample or a series of samples from the same population are obtained several times before and after a manipulated event or a naturally occurring event) - considered a type of quasi-experiment
- Cohort study
    - Prospective cohort
    - Retrospective cohort
    - Time series study
- Case-control study
    - Nested case-control study
- Cross-sectional study
    - Community survey (a type of cross-sectional study)

When choosing a _____, many factors must be taken into account. Different types of studies are subject to different types of bias. For example, recall bias is likely to occur in cross-sectional or case-control studies where subjects are asked to recall exposure to risk factors.

a. Study design
c. 180SearchAssistant
b. Longitudinal studies
d. Power III

14. A _____ in programming languages is an attribute of a data which tells the computer (and the programmer) something about the kind of data it is. This involves setting constraints on the datum, such as what values it can take and what operations may be performed upon it.

In a broad sense, a _____ defines a set of values and the allowable operations on those values.

a. 6-3-5 Brainwriting
c. Power III
b. Data type
d. 180SearchAssistant

Chapter 16. Fundamentals of Data Analysis

15. In statistics, analysis of variance (_____) is a collection of statistical models, and their associated procedures, in which the observed variance is partitioned into components due to different explanatory variables. In its simplest form _____ gives a statistical test of whether the means of several groups are all equal, and therefore generalizes Student's two-sample t-test to more than two groups.

There are three conceptual classes of such models:

1. Fixed-effects models assumes that the data came from normal populations which may differ only in their means. (Model 1)
2. Random effects models assume that the data describe a hierarchy of different populations whose differences are constrained by the hierarchy. (Model 2)
3. Mixed-effect models describe situations where both fixed and random effects are present. (Model 3)

In practice, there are several types of _____ depending on the number of treatments and the way they are applied to the subjects in the experiment:

- One-way _____ is used to test for differences among two or more independent groups. Typically, however, the one-way _____ is used to test for differences among at least three groups, since the two-group case can be covered by a T-test (Gossett, 1908.)

a. ACNielsen
b. ANOVA
c. ADTECH
d. AMAX

16. In statistics, _____ is a collection of statistical models, and their associated procedures, in which the observed variance is partitioned into components due to different explanatory variables. The initial techniques of the _____ were developed by the statistician and geneticist R. A. Fisher in the 1920s and 1930s, and is sometimes known as Fisher's ANOVA or Fisher's _____, due to the use of Fisher's F-distribution as part of the test of statistical significance.

There are three conceptual classes of such models:

1. Fixed-effects models assumes that the data came from normal populations which may differ only in their means. (Model 1)
2. Random effects models assume that the data describe a hierarchy of different populations whose differences are constrained by the hierarchy. (Model 2)
3. Mixed-effect models describe situations where both fixed and random effects are present. (Model 3)

In practice, there are several types of ANOVA depending on the number of treatments and the way they are applied to the subjects in the experiment:

- One-way ANOVA is used to test for differences among two or more independent groups. Typically, however, the One-way ANOVA is used to test for differences among at least three groups, since the two-group case can be covered by a T-test (Gossett, 1908.)

a. Arithmetic mean	b. Interval estimation
c. ACNielsen	d. Analysis of variance

17. A _____ is any statistical hypothesis test in which the test statistic has a chi-square distribution when the null hypothesis is true, or any in which the probability distribution of the test statistic (assuming the null hypothesis is true) can be made to approximate a chi-square distribution as closely as desired by making the sample size large enough.

Some examples of chi-squared tests where the chi-square distribution is only approximately valid:

- Pearson's _____, also known as the chi-square goodness-of-fit test or _____ for independence. When mentioned without any modifiers or without other precluding context, this test is usually understood.
- Yates' _____, also known as Yates' correction for continuity.
- Mantel-Haenszel _____.
- Linear-by-linear association _____.
- The portmanteau test in time-series analysis, testing for the presence of autocorrelation
- Likelihood-ratio tests in general statistical modelling, for testing whether there is evidence of the need to move from a simple model to a more complicated one (where the simple model is nested within the complicated one.)

One case where the distribution of the test statistic is an exact chi-square distribution is the test that the variance of a normally-distributed population has a given value based on a sample variance. Such a test is uncommon in practice because values of variances to test against are seldom known exactly.

If a sample of size n is taken from a population having a normal distribution, then there is a well-known result which allows a test to be made of whether the variance of the population has a pre-determined value.

a. Randomization	b. Confounding variables
c. Chi-square test	d. Type I error

18. _____ is a broad label that refers to any individuals or households that use goods and services generated within the economy. The concept of a _____ is used in different contexts, so that the usage and significance of the term may vary.

A _____ is a person who uses any product or service.

a. 180SearchAssistant	b. 6-3-5 Brainwriting
c. Power III	d. Consumer

19. In statistics, _____ is used for two things;

Chapter 16. Fundamentals of Data Analysis

- to construct a simple formula that will predict what value will occur for a quantity of interest when other related variables take given values.
- to allow a test to be made of whether a given variable does have an effect on a quantity of interest in situations where there may be many related variables.

In both cases, several sets of outcomes are available for the quantity of interest together with the related variables.

_____ is a form of regression analysis in which the relationship between one or more independent variables and another variable, called the dependent variable, is modelled by a least squares function, called a _____ equation. This function is a linear combination of one or more model parameters, called regression coefficients. A _____ equation with one independent variable represents a straight line when the predicted value (i.e. the dependant variable from the regression equation) is plotted against the independent variable: this is called a simple _____.

a. Descriptive statistics
b. Heteroskedastic
c. Sample size
d. Linear regression

20. _____ is a statistical method involving the selection of elements from an ordered sampling frame. The most common form of _____ is an equal-probability method, in which every k^{th} element in the frame is selected, where k, the sampling interval (sometimes known as the 'skip'), is calculated as:

sample size (n) = population size (N) /k

Using this procedure each element in the population has a known and equal probability of selection. This makes _____ functionally similar to simple random sampling.

a. Power III
b. 180SearchAssistant
c. Systematic sampling
d. Selection bias

21. _____ is that part of statistical practice concerned with the selection of individual observations intended to yield some knowledge about a population of concern, especially for the purposes of statistical inference. Each observation measures one or more properties (weight, location, etc.) of an observable entity enumerated to distinguish objects or individuals.
a. Richard Buckminster 'Bucky' Fuller
b. AStore
c. Sports Marketing Group
d. Sampling

22. An example of a repeated measures _____ would be if one group were pre- and post-tested. (This example occurs in education quite frequently.) If a teacher wanted to examine the effect of a new set of textbooks on student achievement, (s)he could test the class at the beginning of the year (pretest) and at the end of the year (posttest.)
a. Statistically significant
b. T-Test
c. Moving average
d. Null hypothesis

Chapter 16. Fundamentals of Data Analysis

23. In probability theory and statistics, the _____ of a random variable, probability distribution, or sample is a measure of statistical dispersion, averaging the squared distance of its possible values from the expected value (mean.) Whereas the mean is a way to describe the location of a distribution, the _____ is a way to capture its scale or degree of being spread out. The unit of _____ is the square of the unit of the original variable.

   a. Standard deviation
   b. Sample size
   c. Variance
   d. Correlation

24. A _____ is any statistical test for which the distribution of the test statistic under the null hypothesis can be approximated by a normal distribution. Since many test statistics are approximately normally distributed for large samples (due to the central limit theorem), many statistical tests can be performed as approximate _____s if the sample size is not too small. In addition, some statistical tests such as comparisons of means between two samples, or a comparison of the mean of one sample to a given constant, are exact _____s under certain assumptions.

   a. Null hypothesis
   b. Z-Test
   c. Confounding variables
   d. Sample size

25. In statistics, _____ analysis, introduced by Harold Hotelling, is a way of making sense of cross-covariance matrices.

    Given two column vectors $X = (x_1, \ldots, x_n)'$ and $Y = (y_1, \ldots, y_m)'$ of random variables with finite second moments, one may define the cross-covariance $\Sigma_{12} = \text{cov}(X, Y)$ to be the $n \times m$ matrix whose (i,j) entry is the covariance $\text{cov}(x_i, y_j)$.

    _____ analysis seeks vectors a and b such that the random variables a'X and b'Y maximize the correlation $\rho = \text{cor}(a'X, b'Y)$.

   a. Sample covariance
   b. Canonical correlation
   c. 180SearchAssistant
   d. Power III

26. In statistics, _____, introduced by Harold Hotelling, is a way of making sense of cross-covariance matrices.

    Given two column vectors $X = (x_1, \ldots, x_n)'$ and $Y = (y_1, \ldots, y_m)'$ of random variables with finite second moments, one may define the cross-covariance $\Sigma_{12} = \text{cov}(X, Y)$ to be the $n \times m$ matrix whose (i,j) entry is the covariance $\text{cov}(x_i, y_j)$.

    _____ seeks vectors a and b such that the random variables a'X and b'Y maximize the correlation $\rho = \text{cor}(a'X, b'Y)$.

   a. Canonical correlation analysis
   b. Sample covariance
   c. 180SearchAssistant
   d. Power III

Chapter 16. Fundamentals of Data Analysis

27. '_____' is a class of statistical techniques that can be applied to data that exhibit 'natural' groupings. _____ sorts through the raw data and groups them into clusters. A cluster is a group of relatively homogeneous cases or observations.
    a. Structure mining
    b. Power III
    c. 180SearchAssistant
    d. Cluster analysis

28. In algebra, the _____ of a polynomial with real or complex coefficients is a certain expression in the coefficients of the polynomial which is equal to zero if and only if the polynomial has a multiple root (i.e. a root with multiplicity greater than one) in the complex numbers. For example, the _____ of the quadratic polynomial

$$ax^2 + bx + c \text{ is } b^2 - 4ac.$$

The _____ of the cubic polynomial

$$ax^3 + bx^2 + cx + d \text{ is } b^2c^2 - 4ac^3 - 4b^3d - 27a^2d^2 + 18abcd.$$

   a. Lifestyle center
   b. Consumption Map
   c. Flighting
   d. Discriminant

29. Linear _____ and the related Fisher's linear discriminant are methods used in statistics and machine learning to find the linear combination of features which best separate two or more classes of objects or events. The resulting combination may be used as a linear classifier, or, more commonly, for dimensionality reduction before later classification.

   LDiscriminant analysis is closely related to ANOVA (analysis of variance) and regression analysis, which also attempt to express one dependent variable as a linear combination of other features or measurements.

   a. Geodemographic segmentation
   b. Linear discriminant analysis
   c. Multiple discriminant analysis
   d. Discriminant analysis

30. _____ is a statistical method used to describe variability among observed variables in terms of fewer unobserved variables called factors. The observed variables are modeled as linear combinations of the factors, plus 'error' terms. The information gained about the interdependencies can be used later to reduce the set of variables in a dataset.
    a. Semantic differential
    b. Likert scale
    c. Power III
    d. Factor analysis

31. In probability theory and statistics, _____ indicates the strength and direction of a linear relationship between two random variables. That is in contrast with the usage of the term in colloquial speech, denoting any relationship, not necessarily linear. In general statistical usage, _____ or co-relation refers to the departure of two random variables from independence.
    a. Mean
    b. Probability
    c. Correlation
    d. Frequency distribution

32. _____ is a statistical technique used in market research to determine how people value different features that make up an individual product or service.

The objective of _____ is to determine what combination of a limited number of attributes is most influential on respondent choice or decision making. A controlled set of potential products or services is shown to respondents and by analyzing how they make preferences between these products, the implicit valuation of the individual elements making up the product or service can be determined.

a. Semantic differential
c. Power III
b. Conjoint analysis
d. Likert scale

33. _____ is a set of related statistical techniques often used in information visualization for exploring similarities or dissimilarities in data. MDS is a special case of ordination. An MDS algorithm starts with a matrix of item-item similarities, then assigns a location to each item in N-dimensional space, where N is specified a priori.

a. Situational theory of publics
c. Cocooning
b. Convenience
d. Multidimensional scaling

34. In statistics, _____ is a collective name for techniques for the modeling and analysis of numerical data consisting of values of a dependent variable and of one or more independent variables The dependent variable in the regression equation is modeled as a function of the independent variables, corresponding parameters, and an error term. The error term is treated as a random variable.

a. Variance inflation factor
c. Stepwise regression
b. Multicollinearity
d. Regression analysis

Chapter 17. Hypothesis Testing: Basic Concepts and Tests of Associations

1. In statistics, _____ is a collection of statistical models, and their associated procedures, in which the observed variance is partitioned into components due to different explanatory variables. The initial techniques of the _____ were developed by the statistician and geneticist R. A. Fisher in the 1920s and 1930s, and is sometimes known as Fisher's ANOVA or Fisher's _____, due to the use of Fisher's F-distribution as part of the test of statistical significance.

There are three conceptual classes of such models:

1. Fixed-effects models assumes that the data came from normal populations which may differ only in their means. (Model 1)
2. Random effects models assume that the data describe a hierarchy of different populations whose differences are constrained by the hierarchy. (Model 2)
3. Mixed-effect models describe situations where both fixed and random effects are present. (Model 3)

In practice, there are several types of ANOVA depending on the number of treatments and the way they are applied to the subjects in the experiment:

- One-way ANOVA is used to test for differences among two or more independent groups. Typically, however, the One-way ANOVA is used to test for differences among at least three groups, since the two-group case can be covered by a T-test (Gossett, 1908.)

a. Arithmetic mean
b. Analysis of variance
c. Interval estimation
d. ACNielsen

2. In probability theory and statistics, the _____ of a random variable, probability distribution, or sample is a measure of statistical dispersion, averaging the squared distance of its possible values from the expected value (mean.) Whereas the mean is a way to describe the location of a distribution, the _____ is a way to capture its scale or degree of being spread out. The unit of _____ is the square of the unit of the original variable.

a. Correlation
b. Sample size
c. Standard deviation
d. Variance

3. The _____ and the null hypothesis are the two rival hypotheses whose likelihoods are compared by a statistical hypothesis test. Usually the _____ is the possibility that an observed effect is genuine and the null hypothesis is the rival possibility that it has resulted from chance.

The classical (or frequentist) approach is to calculate the probability that the observed effect (or one more extreme) will occur if the null hypothesis is true.

a. ACNielsen
b. Analysis of variance
c. Interval estimation
d. Alternative hypothesis

4. The _____ of a test is a traditional frequentist statistical hypothesis testing concept. In simple cases, it is defined as the probability of making a decision to reject the null hypothesis when the null hypothesis is actually true (a decision known as a Type I error, or 'false positive determination'.) The decision is often made using the p-value: if the p-value is less than the _____, then the null hypothesis is rejected.

a. Standard deviation
b. Statistical hypothesis test
c. Significance level
d. Type I error

Chapter 17. Hypothesis Testing: Basic Concepts and Tests of Associations

5. _____ is one of the four elements of marketing mix. An organization or set of organizations (go-betweens) involved in the process of making a product or service available for use or consumption by a consumer or business user.

The other three parts of the marketing mix are product, pricing, and promotion.

a. Distribution
b. Comparison-Shopping agent
c. Better Living Through Chemistry
d. Japan Advertising Photographers' Association

6. _____ is a way of expressing knowledge or belief that an event will occur or has occurred. In mathematics the concept has been given an exact meaning in _____ theory, that is used extensively in such areas of study as mathematics, statistics, finance, gambling, science, and philosophy to draw conclusions about the likelihood of potential events and the underlying mechanics of complex systems.

a. Data
b. Heteroskedastic
c. Linear regression
d. Probability

7. A personal and cultural _____ is a relative ethic _____, an assumption upon which implementation can be extrapolated. A _____ system is a set of consistent _____s and measures that is soo not true. A principle _____ is a foundation upon which other _____s and measures of integrity are based.

a. Package-on-Package
b. Supreme Court of the United States
c. Perceptual maps
d. Value

8. A _____ is any statistical hypothesis test in which the test statistic has a chi-square distribution when the null hypothesis is true, or any in which the probability distribution of the test statistic (assuming the null hypothesis is true) can be made to approximate a chi-square distribution as closely as desired by making the sample size large enough.

Some examples of chi-squared tests where the chi-square distribution is only approximately valid:

- Pearson's _____, also known as the chi-square goodness-of-fit test or _____ for independence. When mentioned without any modifiers or without other precluding context, this test is usually understood.
- Yates' _____, also known as Yates' correction for continuity.
- Mantel-Haenszel _____.
- Linear-by-linear association _____.
- The portmanteau test in time-series analysis, testing for the presence of autocorrelation
- Likelihood-ratio tests in general statistical modelling, for testing whether there is evidence of the need to move from a simple model to a more complicated one (where the simple model is nested within the complicated one.)

One case where the distribution of the test statistic is an exact chi-square distribution is the test that the variance of a normally-distributed population has a given value based on a sample variance. Such a test is uncommon in practice because values of variances to test against are seldom known exactly.

If a sample of size n is taken from a population having a normal distribution, then there is a well-known result which allows a test to be made of whether the variance of the population has a pre-determined value.

Chapter 17. Hypothesis Testing: Basic Concepts and Tests of Associations 83

a. Type I error
c. Chi-square test
b. Randomization
d. Confounding variables

9. In statistics, the terms _____ and type II error are used to describe possible errors made in a statistical decision process. In 1928, Jerzy Neyman (1894-1981) and Egon Pearson (1895-1980), both eminent statisticians, discussed the problems associated with 'deciding whether or not a particular sample may be judged as likely to have been randomly drawn from a certain population' (1928/1967, p.1): and identified 'two sources of error', namely:

Type I (>α): reject the null-hypothesis when the null-hypothesis is true, and
Type II (>β): fail to reject the null-hypothesis when the null-hypothesis is false

In 1930, they elaborated on these two sources of error, remarking that 'in testing hypotheses two considerations must be kept in view, (1) we must be able to reduce the chance of rejecting a true hypothesis to as low a value as desired; (2) the test must be so devised that it will reject the hypothesis tested when it is likely to be false'

Scientists recognize two different sorts of error:

- Statistical error: the difference between a computed, estimated specified and inherently unpredictable fluctuations in the measurement apparatus or the system being studied.
- Systematic error: the difference between a computed, estimated specified and which, once identified, can usually be eliminated.

Statisticians speak of two significant sorts of statistical error. The context is that there is a 'null hypothesis' which corresponds to a presumed default 'state of nature', e.g., that an individual is free of disease, that an accused is innocent that is, that the individual has the disease, that the accused is guilty, or that the login candidate is an authorized user.

a. Probability sampling
c. Mean
b. Significance level
d. Type I error

10. A _____ is a form of qualitative research in which a group of people are asked about their attitude towards a product, service, concept, advertisement, idea, or packaging. Questions are asked in an interactive group setting where participants are free to talk with other group members.

Ernest Dichter originated the idea of having a 'group therapy' for products and this process is what became known as a _____.

a. Focus group
c. Cross tabulation
b. Logit analysis
d. Marketing research process

11. The _____ is a statistical test used in inference, in which a given statistical hypothesis will be rejected when the value of the statistic is either sufficiently small or sufficiently large. The test is named after the 'tail' of data under the far left and far right of a bell-shaped normal data distribution, or bell curve. However, the terminology is extended to tests relating to distributions other than normal.

a. Varimax rotation
b. Sampling error
c. Power III
d. Two-tailed test

12. In probability theory and statistics, the _____ (or expectation value or mean and for continuous random variables with a density function it is the probability density-weighted integral of the possible values.

The term '_____' can be misleading.

a. AMAX
b. ACNielsen
c. ADTECH
d. Expected value

13. _____ is a mathematical science pertaining to the collection, analysis, interpretation or explanation, and presentation of data. It also provides tools for prediction and forecasting based on data. It is applicable to a wide variety of academic disciplines, from the natural and social sciences to the humanities, government and business.

a. Statistics
b. Median
c. Null hypothesis
d. Type I error

14. _____s are used in open sentences. For instance, in the formula x + 1 = 5, x is a _____ which represents an 'unknown' number. _____s are often represented by letters of the Roman alphabet, or those of other alphabets, such as Greek, and use other special symbols.

a. Personalization
b. Quantitative
c. Book of business
d. Variable

Chapter 18. Hypothesis Testing: Means and Proportions

1. In statistics, _____ is a collection of statistical models, and their associated procedures, in which the observed variance is partitioned into components due to different explanatory variables. The initial techniques of the _____ were developed by the statistician and geneticist R. A. Fisher in the 1920s and 1930s, and is sometimes known as Fisher's ANOVA or Fisher's _____, due to the use of Fisher's F-distribution as part of the test of statistical significance.

There are three conceptual classes of such models:

1. Fixed-effects models assumes that the data came from normal populations which may differ only in their means. (Model 1)
2. Random effects models assume that the data describe a hierarchy of different populations whose differences are constrained by the hierarchy. (Model 2)
3. Mixed-effect models describe situations where both fixed and random effects are present. (Model 3)

In practice, there are several types of ANOVA depending on the number of treatments and the way they are applied to the subjects in the experiment:

- One-way ANOVA is used to test for differences among two or more independent groups. Typically, however, the One-way ANOVA is used to test for differences among at least three groups, since the two-group case can be covered by a T-test (Gossett, 1908.)

a. Arithmetic mean
c. Interval estimation
b. ACNielsen
d. Analysis of variance

2. The _____ is a statistical test used in inference, in which a given statistical hypothesis will be rejected when the value of the statistic is either sufficiently small or sufficiently large. The test is named after the 'tail' of data under the far left and far right of a bell-shaped normal data distribution, or bell curve. However, the terminology is extended to tests relating to distributions other than normal.

a. Varimax rotation
c. Power III
b. Sampling error
d. Two-tailed test

3. In statistics, _____ has two related meanings:

- the arithmetic _____
- the expected value of a random variable, which is also called the population _____.

It is sometimes stated that the '_____' _____s average. This is incorrect if '_____' is taken in the specific sense of 'arithmetic _____' as there are different types of averages: the _____, median, and mode. For instance, average house prices almost always use the median value for the average. These three types of averages are all measures of locations.

a. Standard normal distribution
c. Confidence interval
b. Mean
d. Heteroskedastic

4. In probability theory and statistics, the _____ of a random variable, probability distribution, or sample is a measure of statistical dispersion, averaging the squared distance of its possible values from the expected value (mean.) Whereas the mean is a way to describe the location of a distribution, the _____ is a way to capture its scale or degree of being spread out. The unit of _____ is the square of the unit of the original variable.
   a. Standard deviation
   b. Correlation
   c. Sample size
   d. Variance

5. _____ is a way of expressing knowledge or belief that an event will occur or has occurred. In mathematics the concept has been given an exact meaning in _____ theory, that is used extensively in such areas of study as mathematics, statistics, finance, gambling, science, and philosophy to draw conclusions about the likelihood of potential events and the underlying mechanics of complex systems.
   a. Data
   b. Heteroskedastic
   c. Linear regression
   d. Probability

6. A personal and cultural _____ is a relative ethic _____, an assumption upon which implementation can be extrapolated. A _____ system is a set of consistent _____s and measures that is soo not true. A principle _____ is a foundation upon which other _____s and measures of integrity are based.
   a. Perceptual maps
   b. Supreme Court of the United States
   c. Package-on-Package
   d. Value

7. In statistics, a _____ is an interval estimate of a population parameter. Instead of estimating the parameter by a single value, an interval likely to include the parameter is given. Thus, _____s are used to indicate the reliability of an estimate.
   a. T-test
   b. Sample mean
   c. Linear regression
   d. Confidence interval

8. The _____ of a statistical sample is the number of observations that constitute it. It is typically denoted n, a positive integer (natural number.)

Typically, all else being equal, a larger _____ leads to increased precision in estimates of various properties of the population.

   a. Sample size
   b. Heteroskedastic
   c. Frequency distribution
   d. Data

9. _____ is that part of statistical practice concerned with the selection of individual observations intended to yield some knowledge about a population of concern, especially for the purposes of statistical inference. Each observation measures one or more properties (weight, location, etc.) of an observable entity enumerated to distinguish objects or individuals.
   a. Sampling
   b. AStore
   c. Sports Marketing Group
   d. Richard Buckminster 'Bucky' Fuller

10. _____ in economics and business is the result of an exchange and from that trade we assign a numerical monetary value to a good, service or asset. If I trade 4 apples for an orange, the _____ of an orange is 4 - apples. Inversely, the _____ of an apple is 1/4 oranges.

Chapter 18. Hypothesis Testing: Means and Proportions

a. Pricing
b. Discounts and allowances
c. Price
d. Contribution margin-based pricing

11. In statistical hypothesis testing, the _____ is the probability of obtaining a result at least as extreme as the one that was actually observed, assuming that the null hypothesis is true. The fact that _____s are based on this assumption is crucial to their correct interpretation.

More technically, a _____ of an experiment is a random variable defined over the sample space of the experiment such that its distribution under the null hypothesis is uniform on the interval [0,1].

a. Descriptive statistics
b. Correlation
c. Pearson product-moment correlation coefficient
d. P-Value

12. In statistics, analysis of variance (_____) is a collection of statistical models, and their associated procedures, in which the observed variance is partitioned into components due to different explanatory variables. In its simplest form _____ gives a statistical test of whether the means of several groups are all equal, and therefore generalizes Student's two-sample t-test to more than two groups.

There are three conceptual classes of such models:

1. Fixed-effects models assumes that the data came from normal populations which may differ only in their means. (Model 1)
2. Random effects models assume that the data describe a hierarchy of different populations whose differences are constrained by the hierarchy. (Model 2)
3. Mixed-effect models describe situations where both fixed and random effects are present. (Model 3)

In practice, there are several types of _____ depending on the number of treatments and the way they are applied to the subjects in the experiment:

- One-way _____ is used to test for differences among two or more independent groups. Typically, however, the one-way _____ is used to test for differences among at least three groups, since the two-group case can be covered by a T-test (Gossett, 1908.)

a. ACNielsen
b. ADTECH
c. AMAX
d. ANOVA

13. _____,, is a common tool in the retail industry to create the look of a perfectly stocked store by pulling all of the products on a display or shelf to the front, as well as downstacking all the canned and stacked items. It is also done to keep the store appearing neat and organized.

The workers who face commonly have jobs doing other things in the store such as customer service, stocking shelves, daytime cleaning, bagging and carryouts, etc.

Chapter 18. Hypothesis Testing: Means and Proportions

a. Foviance
c. Customer Experience Analytics

b. Customer Integrated System
d. Facing

14. In statistics, an _____ is a term in a statistical model added when the effect of two or more variables is not simply additive. Such a term reflects that the effect of one variable depends on the values of one or more other variables.

Thus, for a response Y and two variables x_1 and x_2 an additive model would be:

$$Y = ax_1 + bx_2 + \text{error}$$

In contrast to this,

$$Y = ax_1 + bx_2 + c(x_1 \times x_2) + \text{error},$$

is an example of a model with an _____ between variables x_1 and x_2 ('error' refers to the random variable whose value by which y differs from the expected value of y.)

a. AMAX
c. ACNielsen

b. ADTECH
d. Interaction

Chapter 19. Correlation Analysis and Regression Analysis

1. In probability theory and statistics, _____ indicates the strength and direction of a linear relationship between two random variables. That is in contrast with the usage of the term in colloquial speech, denoting any relationship, not necessarily linear. In general statistical usage, _____ or co-relation refers to the departure of two random variables from independence.
    a. Mean
    b. Correlation
    c. Probability
    d. Frequency distribution

2. In statistics, _____ is used for two things;

    - to construct a simple formula that will predict what value will occur for a quantity of interest when other related variables take given values.
    - to allow a test to be made of whether a given variable does have an effect on a quantity of interest in situations where there may be many related variables.

    In both cases, several sets of outcomes are available for the quantity of interest together with the related variables.

    _____ is a form of regression analysis in which the relationship between one or more independent variables and another variable, called the dependent variable, is modelled by a least squares function, called a _____ equation. This function is a linear combination of one or more model parameters, called regression coefficients. A _____ equation with one independent variable represents a straight line when the predicted value (i.e. the dependant variable from the regression equation) is plotted against the independent variable: this is called a simple _____.

    a. Linear regression
    b. Sample size
    c. Heteroskedastic
    d. Descriptive statistics

3. In statistics, the _____ is a common measure of the correlation (linear dependence) between two variables X and Y. It is very widely used in the sciences as a measure of the strength of linear dependence between two variables, giving a value somewhere between +1 and -1 inclusive. It was first introduced by Francis Galton in the 1880s, and named after Karl Pearson.

    In accordance with the usual convention, when calculated for an entire population, the Pearson product-moment correlation is typically designated by the analogous Greek letter, which in this case is ρ.

    a. Pearson product-moment correlation coefficient
    b. Median
    c. Standard deviation
    d. Control chart

4. In statistics, _____ is a collective name for techniques for the modeling and analysis of numerical data consisting of values of a dependent variable and of one or more independent variables The dependent variable in the regression equation is modeled as a function of the independent variables, corresponding parameters, and an error term. The error term is treated as a random variable.
    a. Stepwise regression
    b. Variance inflation factor
    c. Regression analysis
    d. Multicollinearity

Chapter 19. Correlation Analysis and Regression Analysis

5. 'Speaking generally, properties are those physical quantities which directly describe the physical attributes of the system; _____s are those combinations of the properties which suffice to determine the response of the system. Properties can have all sorts of dimensions, depending upon the system being considered; _____s are dimensionless, or have the dimension of time or its reciprocal.'

The term can also be used in engineering contexts, however, as it is typically used in the physical sciences.

When the terms formal _____ and actual _____ are used, they generally correspond with the definitions used in computer science.

a. 180SearchAssistant
b. Parameter
c. 6-3-5 Brainwriting
d. Power III

6. In statistics, _____ has two related meanings:

- the arithmetic _____
- the expected value of a random variable, which is also called the population _____.

It is sometimes stated that the '_____' _____s average. This is incorrect if '_____' is taken in the specific sense of 'arithmetic _____' as there are different types of averages: the _____, median, and mode. For instance, average house prices almost always use the median value for the average. These three types of averages are all measures of locations.

a. Heteroskedastic
b. Mean
c. Confidence interval
d. Standard normal distribution

7. In statistics, the _____ or _____ of an estimator is one of many ways to quantify the amount by which an estimator differs from the true value of the quantity being estimated. As a loss function, _____ is called squared error loss. _____ measures the average of the square of the 'error.' The error is the amount by which the estimator differs from the quantity to be estimated.

a. 180SearchAssistant
b. Mean squared error
c. Power III
d. 6-3-5 Brainwriting

8. _____s are used in open sentences. For instance, in the formula x + 1 = 5, x is a _____ which represents an 'unknown' number. _____s are often represented by letters of the Roman alphabet, or those of other alphabets, such as Greek, and use other special symbols.

a. Personalization
b. Quantitative
c. Variable
d. Book of business

9. A _____ is a statement or claim that a particular event will occur in the future in more certain terms than a forecast. The etymology of this word is Latin . In regards to predicting the future Howard H. Stevenson Says, '_____ is at least two things: Important and hard.' Important, because we have to act, and hard because we have to realize the future we want, and what is the best way to get there.

a. 180SearchAssistant
b. 6-3-5 Brainwriting
c. Power III
d. Prediction

Chapter 19. Correlation Analysis and Regression Analysis

10. A _____ is a method of making statistical decisions using experimental data. It is sometimes called confirmatory data analysis, in contrast to exploratory data analysis. In frequency probability, these decisions are almost always made using null-hypothesis tests; that is, ones that answer the question Assuming that the null hypothesis is true, what is the probability of observing a value for the test statistic that is at least as extreme as the value that was actually observed? One use of hypothesis testing is deciding whether experimental results contain enough information to cast doubt on conventional wisdom.

a. Standard normal distribution
b. Probability sampling
c. Statistical hypothesis test
d. Frequency distribution

11. _____ is a statistical phenomenon in which two or more predictor variables in a multiple regression model are highly correlated. In this situation the coefficient estimates may change erratically in response to small changes in the model or the data. _____ does not reduce the predictive power or reliability of the model as a whole; it only affects calculations regarding individual predictors.

a. Multicollinearity
b. Variance inflation factor
c. Regression analysis
d. Stepwise regression

12. In statistics, _____ includes regression models in which the choice of predictive variables is carried out by an automatic procedure. Usually, this takes the form of a sequence of F-tests, but other techniques are possible, such as t-tests, adjusted R-square, Akaike information criterion, Bayesian information criterion, Mallows' Cp, or false discovery rate. In this example from engineering, necessity and sufficiency are usually determined by F-tests.

a. Stepwise regression
b. Multicollinearity
c. Variance inflation factor
d. Regression analysis

13. In statistics, an _____ is a term in a statistical model added when the effect of two or more variables is not simply additive. Such a term reflects that the effect of one variable depends on the values of one or more other variables.

Thus, for a response Y and two variables x_1 and x_2 an additive model would be:

$$Y = ax_1 + bx_2 + \text{error}$$

In contrast to this,

$$Y = ax_1 + bx_2 + c(x_1 \times x_2) + \text{error},$$

is an example of a model with an _____ between variables x_1 and x_2 ('error' refers to the random variable whose value by which y differs from the expected value of y.)

a. AMAX
b. ACNielsen
c. ADTECH
d. Interaction

14. _____ is a mathematical tool for finding repeating patterns, such as the presence of a periodic signal which has been buried under noise, or identifying the missing fundamental frequency in a signal implied by its harmonic frequencies. It is used frequently in signal processing for analyzing functions or series of values, such as time domain signals. Informally, it is the similarity between observations as a function of the time separation between them.

a. Autocorrelation b. AMAX
c. ACNielsen d. ADTECH

15. In psychometrics, _____ is the extent to which a score on a scale or test predicts scores on some criterion measure.

For example, the validity of a cognitive test for job performance is the correlation between test scores and, for example, supervisor performance ratings. Such a cognitive test would have _____ if the observed correlation were statistically significant.

a. Convergent validity b. Discriminant validity
c. Predictive validity d. Criterion validity

Chapter 20. Discriminant and Canonical Analysis

1. In algebra, the _____ of a polynomial with real or complex coefficients is a certain expression in the coefficients of the polynomial which is equal to zero if and only if the polynomial has a multiple root (i.e. a root with multiplicity greater than one) in the complex numbers. For example, the _____ of the quadratic polynomial

$$ax^2 + bx + c \text{ is } b^2 - 4ac.$$

The _____ of the cubic polynomial

$$ax^3 + bx^2 + cx + d \text{ is } b^2c^2 - 4ac^3 - 4b^3d - 27a^2d^2 + 18abcd.$$

a. Discriminant
b. Flighting
c. Lifestyle center
d. Consumption Map

2. Linear _____ and the related Fisher's linear discriminant are methods used in statistics and machine learning to find the linear combination of features which best separate two or more classes of objects or events. The resulting combination may be used as a linear classifier, or, more commonly, for dimensionality reduction before later classification.

LDiscriminant analysis is closely related to ANOVA (analysis of variance) and regression analysis, which also attempt to express one dependent variable as a linear combination of other features or measurements.

a. Linear discriminant analysis
b. Multiple discriminant analysis
c. Geodemographic segmentation
d. Discriminant analysis

3. In statistics, _____ is used for two things;

- to construct a simple formula that will predict what value will occur for a quantity of interest when other related variables take given values.
- to allow a test to be made of whether a given variable does have an effect on a quantity of interest in situations where there may be many related variables.

In both cases, several sets of outcomes are available for the quantity of interest together with the related variables.

_____ is a form of regression analysis in which the relationship between one or more independent variables and another variable, called the dependent variable, is modelled by a least squares function, called a _____ equation. This function is a linear combination of one or more model parameters, called regression coefficients. A _____ equation with one independent variable represents a straight line when the predicted value (i.e. the dependant variable from the regression equation) is plotted against the independent variable: this is called a simple _____.

a. Sample size
b. Descriptive statistics
c. Heteroskedastic
d. Linear regression

Chapter 20. Discriminant and Canonical Analysis

4. In probability theory and statistics, _____ indicates the strength and direction of a linear relationship between two random variables. That is in contrast with the usage of the term in colloquial speech, denoting any relationship, not necessarily linear. In general statistical usage, _____ or co-relation refers to the departure of two random variables from independence.
   - a. Frequency distribution
   - b. Mean
   - c. Probability
   - d. Correlation

5. In statistics, _____ is a generalization of linear discriminant analysis.
   - a. Discriminant analysis
   - b. Linear discriminant analysis
   - c. Principal component analysis
   - d. Multiple discriminant analysis

6. In statistics, _____ analysis, introduced by Harold Hotelling, is a way of making sense of cross-covariance matrices.

    Given two column vectors $X = (x_1, \ldots, x_n)'$ and $Y = (y_1, \ldots, y_m)'$ of random variables with finite second moments, one may define the cross-covariance $\Sigma_{12} = \operatorname{cov}(X, Y)$ to be the $n \times m$ matrix whose (i,j) entry is the covariance $\operatorname{cov}(x_i, y_j)$.

    _____ analysis seeks vectors a and b such that the random variables a'X and b'Y maximize the correlation $\rho = \operatorname{cor}(a'X, b'Y)$.

   - a. Power III
   - b. Sample covariance
   - c. 180SearchAssistant
   - d. Canonical correlation

7. In statistics, _____, introduced by Harold Hotelling, is a way of making sense of cross-covariance matrices.

    Given two column vectors $X = (x_1, \ldots, x_n)'$ and $Y = (y_1, \ldots, y_m)'$ of random variables with finite second moments, one may define the cross-covariance $\Sigma_{12} = \operatorname{cov}(X, Y)$ to be the $n \times m$ matrix whose (i,j) entry is the covariance $\operatorname{cov}(x_i, y_j)$.

    _____ seeks vectors a and b such that the random variables a'X and b'Y maximize the correlation $\rho = \operatorname{cor}(a'X, b'Y)$.

   - a. Sample covariance
   - b. Power III
   - c. 180SearchAssistant
   - d. Canonical correlation analysis

Chapter 21. Factor and Cluster Analysis

1. _____ is a statistical method used to describe variability among observed variables in terms of fewer unobserved variables called factors. The observed variables are modeled as linear combinations of the factors, plus 'error' terms. The information gained about the interdependencies can be used later to reduce the set of variables in a dataset.
    a. Likert scale
    b. Power III
    c. Semantic differential
    d. Factor analysis

2. _____ involves a mathematical procedure that transforms a number of possibly correlated variables into a smaller number of uncorrelated variables called principal components. The first principal component accounts for as much of the variability in the data as possible, and each succeeding component accounts for as much of the remaining variability as possible. Depending on the field of application, it is also named the discrete Karhunen-Loève transform (KLT), the Hotelling transform or proper orthogonal decomposition (POD.)
    a. Geodemographic segmentation
    b. Principal component analysis
    c. Multiple discriminant analysis
    d. Discriminant analysis

3. _____ is a change of coordinates used in principal component analysis that maximizes the sum of the variance of the loading vectors. That is, it seeks a basis such that most economically represents each individual--that each individual can be well described by a linear combination of only a few basis functions.

Suggested by Henry Felix Kaiser in 1958, it is a popular scheme for orthogonal rotation which cleans up the factors as follows: 'for each factor, high loadings (correlations) will result for a few variables; the rest will be near zero.'

_____ is often used in surveys to see how groupings of questions (items) measure the same concept.

    a. Varimax rotation
    b. Power III
    c. Two-tailed test
    d. Sampling error

4. In probability theory and statistics, the _____ of a random variable, probability distribution, or sample is a measure of statistical dispersion, averaging the squared distance of its possible values from the expected value (mean.) Whereas the mean is a way to describe the location of a distribution, the _____ is a way to capture its scale or degree of being spread out. The unit of _____ is the square of the unit of the original variable.
    a. Standard deviation
    b. Variance
    c. Correlation
    d. Sample size

5. '_____' is a class of statistical techniques that can be applied to data that exhibit 'natural' groupings. _____ sorts through the raw data and groups them into clusters. A cluster is a group of relatively homogeneous cases or observations.
    a. Power III
    b. Structure mining
    c. 180SearchAssistant
    d. Cluster analysis

6. In mathematics, the _____ or Euclidean metric is the 'ordinary' distance between two points that one would measure with a ruler, which can be proven by repeated application of the Pythagorean theorem. By using this formula as distance, Euclidean space becomes a metric space (even a Hilbert space.) The associated norm is called the Euclidean norm.
    a. AMAX
    b. ADTECH
    c. Euclidean distance
    d. ACNielsen

Chapter 21. Factor and Cluster Analysis

7. _____ is the assignment of objects into groups (called clusters) so that objects from the same cluster are more similar to each other than objects from different clusters. Often similarity is assessed according to a distance measure. _____ is a common technique for statistical data analysis, which is used in many fields, including machine learning, data mining, pattern recognition, image analysis and bioinformatics.

   a. Comparison-Shopping agent
   b. Developed country
   c. Just-In-Case
   d. Clustering

8. In mathematics, an _____, or central tendency of a data set refers to a measure of the 'middle' or 'expected' value of the data set. There are many different descriptive statistics that can be chosen as a measurement of the central tendency of the data items.

An _____ is a single value that is meant to typify a list of values.

   a. ACNielsen
   b. AMAX
   c. ADTECH
   d. Average

9. In genetics _____ is defined as the state in which two loci are so close together that alleles of these loci are virtually never separated by crossing over. During reproduction, chromosomes on the same chromosome pair, exchange sections of DNA. As a result, genes that were originally on the same chromosome can finish up on different chromosomes - genetic recombination.

   a. Power III
   b. F-statistics
   c. 180SearchAssistant
   d. Complete linkage

10. _____ is systematic determination of merit, worth, and significance of something or someone using criteria against a set of standards. _____ often is used to characterize and appraise subjects of interest in a wide range of human enterprises, including the arts, criminal justice, foundations and non-profit organizations, government, health care, and other human services.

Depending on the topic of interest, there are professional groups which look to the quality and rigor of the _____ process.

   a. Evaluation
   b. AMAX
   c. ACNielsen
   d. ADTECH

11. _____ or statistical induction comprises the use of statistics to make inferences concerning some unknown aspect of a population. It is distinguished from descriptive statistics.

Two schools of _____ are frequency probability and Bayesian inference.

   a. Moving average
   b. Probability sampling
   c. Standard score
   d. Statistical inference

Chapter 22. Multidimensional Scaling and Conjoint Analysis

1. _____ is a set of related statistical techniques often used in information visualization for exploring similarities or dissimilarities in data. MDS is a special case of ordination. An MDS algorithm starts with a matrix of item-item similarities, then assigns a location to each item in N-dimensional space, where N is specified a priori.

   a. Situational theory of publics
   b. Cocooning
   c. Convenience
   d. Multidimensional scaling

2. Perceptual mapping is a graphics technique used by asset marketers that attempts to visually display the perceptions of customers or potential customers. Typically the position of a product, product line, brand, or company is displayed relative to their competition.

   _____ can have any number of dimensions but the most common is two dimensions.

   a. Perceptual maps
   b. Comparison-Shopping agent
   c. Developed country
   d. Retail floor planning

3. _____ is a statistical method used to describe variability among observed variables in terms of fewer unobserved variables called factors. The observed variables are modeled as linear combinations of the factors, plus 'error' terms. The information gained about the interdependencies can be used later to reduce the set of variables in a dataset.

   a. Factor analysis
   b. Power III
   c. Likert scale
   d. Semantic differential

4. In algebra, the _____ of a polynomial with real or complex coefficients is a certain expression in the coefficients of the polynomial which is equal to zero if and only if the polynomial has a multiple root (i.e. a root with multiplicity greater than one) in the complex numbers. For example, the _____ of the quadratic polynomial

   $$ax^2 + bx + c \text{ is } b^2 - 4ac.$$

   The _____ of the cubic polynomial

   $$ax^3 + bx^2 + cx + d \text{ is } b^2c^2 - 4ac^3 - 4b^3d - 27a^2d^2 + 18abcd.$$

   a. Flighting
   b. Consumption Map
   c. Lifestyle center
   d. Discriminant

5. Linear _____ and the related Fisher's linear discriminant are methods used in statistics and machine learning to find the linear combination of features which best separate two or more classes of objects or events. The resulting combination may be used as a linear classifier, or, more commonly, for dimensionality reduction before later classification.

   LDiscriminant analysis is closely related to ANOVA (analysis of variance) and regression analysis, which also attempt to express one dependent variable as a linear combination of other features or measurements.

   a. Linear discriminant analysis
   b. Discriminant analysis
   c. Multiple discriminant analysis
   d. Geodemographic segmentation

Chapter 22. Multidimensional Scaling and Conjoint Analysis

6. _____ is a multivariate statistical technique developed by Jean-Paul Benzécri that is conceptually similar to principal components analysis, but scales the data (which must be positive) so that rows and columns are treated equivalently. It is traditionally applied to contingency tables. _____ decomposes the Chi-square statistic associated to this table into orthogonal factors.
   a. Discriminant analysis
   b. Correspondence analysis
   c. Principal component analysis
   d. Geodemographic segmentation

7. _____ is systematic determination of merit, worth, and significance of something or someone using criteria against a set of standards. _____ often is used to characterize and appraise subjects of interest in a wide range of human enterprises, including the arts, criminal justice, foundations and non-profit organizations, government, health care, and other human services.

   Depending on the topic of interest, there are professional groups which look to the quality and rigor of the _____ process.

   a. AMAX
   b. Evaluation
   c. ACNielsen
   d. ADTECH

8. A personal and cultural _____ is a relative ethic _____, an assumption upon which implementation can be extrapolated. A _____ system is a set of consistent _____s and measures that is soo not true. A principle _____ is a foundation upon which other _____s and measures of integrity are based.
   a. Supreme Court of the United States
   b. Value
   c. Package-on-Package
   d. Perceptual maps

9. _____ refer to a collection of facts usually collected as the result of experience, observation or experiment or a set of premises. This may consist of numbers, words particularly as measurements or observations of a set of variables. _____ are often viewed as a lowest level of abstraction from which information and knowledge are derived.
   a. Mean
   b. Data
   c. Sample size
   d. Pearson product-moment correlation coefficient

10. _____ is a statistical technique used in market research to determine how people value different features that make up an individual product or service.

    The objective of _____ is to determine what combination of a limited number of attributes is most influential on respondent choice or decision making. A controlled set of potential products or services is shown to respondents and by analyzing how they make preferences between these products, the implicit valuation of the individual elements making up the product or service can be determined.

    a. Likert scale
    b. Conjoint analysis
    c. Semantic differential
    d. Power III

11. _____ is a process of gathering, modeling, and transforming data with the goal of highlighting useful information, suggesting conclusions, and supporting decision making. _____ has multiple facets and approaches, encompassing diverse techniques under a variety of names, in different business, science, and social science domains.

Data mining is a particular _____ technique that focuses on modeling and knowledge discovery for predictive rather than purely descriptive purposes.

a. 180SearchAssistant
b. Data analysis
c. Power III
d. 6-3-5 Brainwriting

Chapter 23. Presenting the Results

1. _____ is a fee paid on borrowed assets. It is the price paid for the use of borrowed money, or, money earned by deposited funds. Assets that are sometimes lent with _____ include money, shares, consumer goods through hire purchase, major assets such as aircraft, and even entire factories in finance lease arrangements.
   a. ACNielsen
   b. AMAX
   c. ADTECH
   d. Interest

2. The _____ is a very large set of interlinked hypertext documents accessed via the Internet. With a Web browser, one can view Web pages that may contain text, images, videos, and other multimedia and navigate between them using hyperlinks. Using concepts from earlier hypertext systems, the _____ was begun in 1992 by the English physicist Sir Tim Berners-Lee, now the Director of the _____ Consortium, and Robert Cailliau, a Belgian computer scientist, while both were working at CERN in Geneva, Switzerland.
   a. Power III
   b. 180SearchAssistant
   c. 6-3-5 Brainwriting
   d. World Wide Web

Chapter 24. Traditional Applications: Product, Price, Distribution, and Promotion

1. In the art of selling, _____ is one stage in a seven stage personal selling process.

In this stage the salesperson takes a qualified prospect through a series of question and answer sessions in order to identify the requirements of the prospect. During this step, the salesperson will attempt to help the buyer identify and quantify a business need or a 'gap' between where the client is today and where they would like to be in the future.

 a. Power III   b. Need identification
 c. Product churning   d. 180SearchAssistant

2. Perceptual mapping is a graphics technique used by asset marketers that attempts to visually display the perceptions of customers or potential customers. Typically the position of a product, product line, brand, or company is displayed relative to their competition.

_____ can have any number of dimensions but the most common is two dimensions.

 a. Retail floor planning   b. Comparison-Shopping agent
 c. Developed country   d. Perceptual maps

3. _____ is a term developed by Eric von Hippel in 1986. His definition for _____ is:

 1. _____s face needs that will be general in a marketplace - but face them months or years before the bulk of that marketplace encounters them, and
 2. _____s are positioned to benefit significantly by obtaining a solution to those needs.

In other words: _____s are users of a product that currently experience needs still unknown to the public and who also benefit greatly if they obtain a solution to these needs.

The _____ Method is a market research tool that may be used by companies and / or individuals seeking to develop breakthrough products. _____ methodology was originally developed by Dr. Eric von Hippel of the Massachusetts Institute of Technology (MIT) and first described in the July 1986 issue of the Journal of Management Science.

 a. 6-3-5 Brainwriting   b. Power III
 c. 180SearchAssistant   d. Lead user

4. _____ is systematic determination of merit, worth, and significance of something or someone using criteria against a set of standards. _____ often is used to characterize and appraise subjects of interest in a wide range of human enterprises, including the arts, criminal justice, foundations and non-profit organizations, government, health care, and other human services.

Depending on the topic of interest, there are professional groups which look to the quality and rigor of the _____ process.

a. AMAX
b. Evaluation
c. ACNielsen
d. ADTECH

5. _____ is defined by the American _____ Association as the activity, set of institutions, and processes for creating, communicating, delivering, and exchanging offerings that have value for customers, clients, partners, and society at large. The term developed from the original meaning which referred literally to going to market, as in shopping, or going to a market to sell goods or services.

_____ practice tends to be seen as a creative industry, which includes advertising, distribution and selling.

a. Customer acquisition management
b. Marketing myopia
c. Product naming
d. Marketing

6. A _____, in the field of business and marketing, is a geographic region or demographic group used to gauge the viability of a product or service in the mass market prior to a wide scale roll-out. The criteria used to judge the acceptability of a _____ region or group include:

1. a population that is demographically similar to the proposed target market; and
2. relative isolation from densely populated media markets so that advertising to the test audience can be efficient and economical.

The _____ ideally aims to duplicate 'everything' - promotion and distribution as well as `product' - on a smaller scale. The technique replicates, typically in one area, what is planned to occur in a national launch; and the results are very carefully monitored, so that they can be extrapolated to projected national results. The `area' may be any one of the following:

- Television area
- Test town
- Residential neighborhood
- Test site

A number of decisions have to be taken about any _____:

- Which _____?
- What is to be tested?
- How long a test?
- What are the success criteria?

The simple go or no-go decision, together with the related reduction of risk, is normally the main justification for the expense of _____s. At the same time, however, such _____s can be used to test specific elements of a new product's marketing mix; possibly the version of the product itself, the promotional message and media spend, the distribution channels and the price.

Chapter 24. Traditional Applications: Product, Price, Distribution, and Promotion 103

a. 180SearchAssistant
b. Power III
c. Preadolescence
d. Test market

7. _____ generally refers to a list of all planned expenses and revenues. It is a plan for saving and spending. A _____ is an important concept in microeconomics, which uses a _____ line to illustrate the trade-offs between two or more goods.
a. Budget
b. Power III
c. 6-3-5 Brainwriting
d. 180SearchAssistant

8. In economics, business, retail, and accounting, a _____ is the value of money that has been used up to produce something, and hence is not available for use anymore. In economics, a _____ is an alternative that is given up as a result of a decision. In business, the _____ may be one of acquisition, in which case the amount of money expended to acquire it is counted as _____.
a. Variable cost
b. Fixed costs
c. Transaction cost
d. Cost

9. Competitiveness is a comparative concept of the ability and performance of a firm, sub-sector or country to sell and supply goods and/or services in a given market. Although widely used in economics and business management, the usefulness of the concept, particularly in the context of national competitiveness, is vigorously disputed by economists, such as Paul Krugman .

The term may also be applied to markets, where it is used to refer to the extent to which the market structure may be regarded as perfectly _____.

a. Geographical pricing
b. Customs union
c. Free trade zone
d. Competitive

10. _____ is, in very basic words, a position a firm occupies against its competitors.

According to Michael Porter, the three methods for creating a sustainable _____ are through:

1. Cost leadership - Cost advantage occurs when a firm delivers the same services as its competitors but at a lower cost;

2.

a. 6-3-5 Brainwriting
b. 180SearchAssistant
c. Power III
d. Competitive advantage

11. _____ refer to a collection of facts usually collected as the result of experience, observation or experiment or a set of premises. This may consist of numbers, words particularly as measurements or observations of a set of variables. _____ are often viewed as a lowest level of abstraction from which information and knowledge are derived.
a. Sample size
b. Mean
c. Data
d. Pearson product-moment correlation coefficient

Chapter 24. Traditional Applications: Product, Price, Distribution, and Promotion

12. _____ is one of the four Ps of the marketing mix. The other three aspects are product, promotion, and place. It is also a key variable in microeconomic price allocation theory.
    a. Price
    b. Relationship based pricing
    c. Competitor indexing
    d. Pricing

13. Procter is a surname, and may also refer to:
    - Bryan Waller Procter (pseud. Barry Cornwall), English poet
    - Goodwin Procter, American law firm
    - _____, consumer products multinational

    a. Procter ' Gamble
    b. Convergent
    c. Flyer
    d. Black PRies

14. _____ is the pricing technique of setting a relatively low initial entry price, often lower than the eventual market price, to attract new customers. The strategy works on the expectation that customers will switch to the new brand because of the lower price. _____ is most commonly associated with a marketing objective of increasing market share or sales volume, rather than to make profit in the short term.
    a. Fee
    b. Competitor indexing
    c. Price war
    d. Penetration pricing

15. _____ is one of the four elements of marketing mix. An organization or set of organizations (go-betweens) involved in the process of making a product or service available for use or consumption by a consumer or business user.

    The other three parts of the marketing mix are product, pricing, and promotion.

    a. Japan Advertising Photographers' Association
    b. Better Living Through Chemistry
    c. Comparison-Shopping agent
    d. Distribution

16. A _____ is a commercial building for storage of goods. _____s are used by manufacturers, importers, exporters, wholesalers, transport businesses, customs, etc. They are usually large plain buildings in industrial areas of cities and towns.
    a. 180SearchAssistant
    b. Power III
    c. 6-3-5 Brainwriting
    d. Warehouse

17. _____ is the imitation of some real thing, state of affairs, or process. The act of simulating something generally entails representing certain key characteristics or behaviors of a selected physical or abstract system.

    _____ is used in many contexts, including the modeling of natural systems or human systems in order to gain insight into their functioning.

    a. Simulation
    b. 180SearchAssistant
    c. Power III
    d. 6-3-5 Brainwriting

Chapter 24. Traditional Applications: Product, Price, Distribution, and Promotion 105

18. _____ is the study of the Earth and its lands, features, inhabitants, and phenomena. A literal translation would be 'to describe or write about the Earth'. The first person to use the word '_____' was Eratosthenes .
   a. Power III
   b. 6-3-5 Brainwriting
   c. Geography
   d. 180SearchAssistant

19. _____ is a set of related statistical techniques often used in information visualization for exploring similarities or dissimilarities in data. MDS is a special case of ordination. An MDS algorithm starts with a matrix of item-item similarities, then assigns a location to each item in N-dimensional space, where N is specified a priori.
   a. Convenience
   b. Multidimensional scaling
   c. Cocooning
   d. Situational theory of publics

20. _____ in economics and business is the result of an exchange and from that trade we assign a numerical monetary value to a good, service or asset. If I trade 4 apples for an orange, the _____ of an orange is 4 - apples. Inversely, the _____ of an apple is 1/4 oranges.
   a. Discounts and allowances
   b. Contribution margin-based pricing
   c. Price
   d. Pricing

21. _____ is the practice of keeping the price of a product or service artificially high in order to encourage favorable perceptions among buyers, based solely on the price. The practice is intended to exploit the (not necessarily justifiable) tendency for buyers to assume that expensive items enjoy an exceptional reputation or represent exceptional quality and distinction.

The use of _____ as either a marketing strategy or a competitive practice depends on certain factors that influence its profitability and sustainability.

   a. Premium pricing
   b. Price maintenance
   c. Price war
   d. Target costing

22. An _____ is a special-purpose computer system designed to perform one or a few dedicated functions, often with real-time computing constraints. It is usually embedded as part of a complete device including hardware and mechanical parts. In contrast, a general-purpose computer, such as a personal computer, can do many different tasks depending on programming.
   a. Embedded system
   b. AMAX
   c. ADTECH
   d. ACNielsen

23. A _____ applies the scientific method to experimentally examine an intervention in the real world (or as many experimental economists like to say, naturally-occurring environments) rather than in the laboratory. _____s, like lab experiments, generally randomize subjects (or other sampling units) into treatment and control groups and compare outcomes between these groups. Clinical trials of pharmaceuticals are one example of _____s.
   a. 180SearchAssistant
   b. Field experiment
   c. Response variable
   d. Power III

Chapter 24. Traditional Applications: Product, Price, Distribution, and Promotion

24. _____ involves disseminating information about a product, product line, brand, or company. It is one of the four key aspects of the marketing mix. (The other three elements are product marketing, pricing, and distribution). P>_____ is generally sub-divided into two parts:

- Above the line _____: Promotion in the media (e.g. TV, radio, newspapers, Internet and Mobile Phones) in which the advertiser pays an advertising agency to place the ad
- Below the line _____: All other _____. Much of this is intended to be subtle enough for the consumer to be unaware that _____ is taking place. E.g. sponsorship, product placement, endorsements, sales _____, merchandising, direct mail, personal selling, public relations, trade shows

a. Cashmere Agency
b. Promotion
c. Bottling lines
d. Davie Brown Index

25. _____ is a form of communication that typically attempts to persuade potential customers to purchase or to consume more of a particular brand of product or service. 'While now central to the contemporary global economy and the reproduction of global production networks, it is only quite recently that _____ has been more than a marginal influence on patterns of sales and production. The formation of modern _____ was intimately bound up with the emergence of new forms of monopoly capitalism around the end of the 19th and beginning of the 20th century as one element in corporate strategies to create, organize and where possible control markets, especially for mass produced consumer goods.

a. ADTECH
b. AMAX
c. Advertising
d. ACNielsen

26. _____ is a specialized form of marketing research conducted to improve the efficiency of advertising. According to MarketConscious.com, 'It may focus on a specific ad or campaign, or may be directed at a more general understanding of how advertising works or how consumers use the information in advertising. It can entail a variety of research approaches, including psychological, sociological, economic, and other perspectives.'

1879 - N.W. Ayer conducts custom research in an attempt to win the advertising business of Nichols-Shepard Co., a manufacturer of agricultural machinery.

a. Electrolux
b. Advertising research
c. INVISTA
d. American Medical Association

27. _____ is a form of social influence. It is the process of guiding people toward the adoption of an idea, attitude, or action by rational and symbolic (though not always logical) means. It is strategy of problem-solving relying on 'appeals' rather than coercion.

a. 180SearchAssistant
b. Persuasion
c. 6-3-5 Brainwriting
d. Power III

28. _____ refers to a business or organization attempting to acquire goods or services to accomplish the goals of the enterprise. Though there are several organizations that attempt to set standards in the _____ process, processes can vary greatly between organizations. Typically the word '_____' is not used interchangeably with the word 'procurement', since procurement typically includes Expediting, Supplier Quality, and Traffic and Logistics (T'L) in addition to _____.

a. Supply chain
b. Supply network
c. Drop shipping
d. Purchasing

Chapter 24. Traditional Applications: Product, Price, Distribution, and Promotion 107

29. A _____ is any kind of medical test performed to aid in the diagnosis or detection of disease. For example:

- to diagnose diseases
- to measure the progress or recovery from disease
- to confirm that a person is free from disease

A drug test can be a specific medical test to acertain the presence of a certain drug in the body (for example, in drug addicts.)

Some medical tests are parts of a simple physical examination which require only simple tools in the hands of a skilled practitioner, and can be performed in an office environment. Some other tests require elaborate equipment used by medical technologists or the use of a sterile operating theatre environment.

a. 180SearchAssistant
c. Power III
b. 6-3-5 Brainwriting
d. Diagnostic test

30. _____ is a broad label that refers to any individuals or households that use goods and services generated within the economy. The concept of a _____ is used in different contexts, so that the usage and significance of the term may vary.

A _____ is a person who uses any product or service.

a. Consumer
c. 6-3-5 Brainwriting
b. 180SearchAssistant
d. Power III

31. A _____ is defined by the International Co-operative Alliance's Statement on the Co-operative Identity as an autonomous association of persons united voluntarily to meet their common economic, social, and cultural needs and aspirations through a jointly-owned and democratically-controlled enterprise. It is a business organization owned and operated by a group of individuals for their mutual benefit. A _____ may also be defined as a business owned and controlled equally by the people who use its services or who work at it.

a. 6-3-5 Brainwriting
c. Cooperative
b. 180SearchAssistant
d. Power III

32. _____ is one of the four aspects of promotional mix. (The other three parts of the promotional mix are advertising, personal selling, and publicity/public relations.) Media and non-media marketing communication are employed for a pre-determined, limited time to increase consumer demand, stimulate market demand or improve product availability.

a. Merchandise
c. Marketing communication
b. New Media Strategies
d. Sales promotion

33. A _____ is a type of business entity in which partners (owners) share with each other the profits or losses of the business undertaking in which all have invested. _____s are often favored over corporations for taxation purposes, as the _____ structure does not generally incur a tax on profits before it is distributed to the partners (i.e. there is no dividend tax levied.) However, depending on the _____ structure and the jurisdiction in which it operates, owners of a _____ may be exposed to greater personal liability than they would as shareholders of a corporation.

a. Brand piracy
c. Competition law
b. Fair Debt Collection Practices Act
d. Partnership

Chapter 25. Contemporary Applications

1. Competitiveness is a comparative concept of the ability and performance of a firm, sub-sector or country to sell and supply goods and/or services in a given market. Although widely used in economics and business management, the usefulness of the concept, particularly in the context of national competitiveness, is vigorously disputed by economists, such as Paul Krugman .

The term may also be applied to markets, where it is used to refer to the extent to which the market structure may be regarded as perfectly _____.

   a. Geographical pricing
   b. Free trade zone
   c. Competitive
   d. Customs union

2. _____ is, in very basic words, a position a firm occupies against its competitors.

According to Michael Porter, the three methods for creating a sustainable _____ are through:

1. Cost leadership - Cost advantage occurs when a firm delivers the same services as its competitors but at a lower cost;

2.

   a. 6-3-5 Brainwriting
   b. 180SearchAssistant
   c. Competitive advantage
   d. Power III

3. _____, in strategic management and marketing, is the percentage or proportion of the total available market or market segment that is being serviced by a company. It can be expressed as a company's sales revenue (from that market) divided by the total sales revenue available in that market. It can also be expressed as a company's unit sales volume (in a market) divided by the total volume of units sold in that market.
   a. Market share
   b. Customer relationship management
   c. Cyberdoc
   d. Demand generation

4. _____ is a form of communication that typically attempts to persuade potential customers to purchase or to consume more of a particular brand of product or service. 'While now central to the contemporary global economy and the reproduction of global production networks, it is only quite recently that _____ has been more than a marginal influence on patterns of sales and production. The formation of modern _____ was intimately bound up with the emergence of new forms of monopoly capitalism around the end of the 19th and beginning of the 20th century as one element in corporate strategies to create, organize and where possible control markets, especially for mass produced consumer goods.
   a. AMAX
   b. ADTECH
   c. ACNielsen
   d. Advertising

5. _____ generally refers to a list of all planned expenses and revenues. It is a plan for saving and spending. A _____ is an important concept in microeconomics, which uses a _____ line to illustrate the trade-offs between two or more goods.
   a. 180SearchAssistant
   b. 6-3-5 Brainwriting
   c. Budget
   d. Power III

6. In economics, business, retail, and accounting, a _____ is the value of money that has been used up to produce something, and hence is not available for use anymore. In economics, a _____ is an alternative that is given up as a result of a decision. In business, the _____ may be one of acquisition, in which case the amount of money expended to acquire it is counted as _____.

a. Transaction cost
b. Variable cost
c. Fixed costs
d. Cost

7. _____ is defined by the American _____ Association as the activity, set of institutions, and processes for creating, communicating, delivering, and exchanging offerings that have value for customers, clients, partners, and society at large. The term developed from the original meaning which referred literally to going to market, as in shopping, or going to a market to sell goods or services.

_____ practice tends to be seen as a creative industry, which includes advertising, distribution and selling.

a. Marketing myopia
b. Customer acquisition management
c. Marketing
d. Product naming

8. The phrase _____, according to the Organization for Economic Co-operation and Development, refers to 'creative work undertaken on a systematic basis in order to increase the stock of knowledge, including knowledge of man, culture and society, and the use of this stock of knowledge to devise new applications [sic]' Though it is questionable that an organization is needed for this definition, as it is quite obvious that _____ refers to the _____ of something.

New product design and development is more often than not a crucial factor in the survival of a company. In an industry that is fast changing, firms must continually revise their design and range of products.

a. Power III
b. 180SearchAssistant
c. Research and development
d. 6-3-5 Brainwriting

9. The general definition of an _____ is an evaluation of a person, organization, system, process, project or product. _____s are performed to ascertain the validity and reliability of information; also to provide an assessment of a system's internal control. The goal of an _____ is to express an opinion on the person/organization/system (etc) in question, under evaluation based on work done on a test basis.

a. Audit
b. ADTECH
c. AMAX
d. ACNielsen

10. A _____ is a collection of symbols, experiences and associations connected with a product, a service, a person or any other artifact or entity.

_____s have become increasingly important components of culture and the economy, now being described as 'cultural accessories and personal philosophies'.

Some people distinguish the psychological aspect of a _____ from the experiential aspect.

a. Brand
b. Store brand
c. Brand equity
d. Brandable software

Chapter 25. Contemporary Applications

11. _____ refers to the marketing effects or outcomes that accrue to a product with its brand name compared with those that would accrue if the same product did not have the brand name . And, at the root of these marketing effects is consumers' knowledge. In other words, consumers' knowledge about a brand makes manufacturers/advertisers respond differently or adopt appropriately adapt measures for the marketing of the brand .

- a. Brand aversion
- b. Product extension
- c. Brand image
- d. Brand equity

12. _____ is a marketing concept that refers to a consumer knowing of a brand's existence; at aggregate (brand) level it refers to the proportion of consumers who know of the brand.

_____ can be measured by showing a consumer the brand and asking whether or not they knew of it beforehand. However, in common market research practice a variety of recognition and recall measures of _____ are employed all of which test the brand name's association to a product category cue, this came about because most market research in the 20th Century was conducted by post or telephone, actually showing the brand to consumers usually required more expensive face-to-face interviews (until web-based interviews became possible.)

- a. Brand equity
- b. Brand awareness
- c. Fitting Group
- d. Brand orientation

13. _____, in marketing, consists of a consumer's commitment to repurchase the brand and can be demonstrated by repeated buying of a product or service or other positive behaviors such as word of mouth advocacy. True _____ implies that the consumer is willing, at least on occasion, to put aside their own desires in the interest of the brand. _____ has been proclaimed by some to be the ultimate goal of marketing.

- a. Brand awareness
- b. Brand implementation
- c. Trade Symbols
- d. Brand loyalty

14. _____ is the process of gathering and analysing information regarding customers; their details and their activities, in order to build deeper and more effective customer relationships and improve strategic decision making.

Consumer Intelligence is also the name of a leading company within the UK Research industry that is referenced in large number of Advertising campaigns by companies such as Asda, Budget Compare The Market, Churchill, Direct Line, MoneySupermarket, Norwich Union and many others.

_____ is a key component of effective Customer Relationship Management, and when effectively implemented it is a rich source of insight into the behaviour and experience of a company's customer base.

- a. Power III
- b. Pop-up ads
- c. Customer intelligence
- d. Project Portfolio Management

15. _____, a business term, is a measure of how products and services supplied by a company meet or surpass customer expectation. It is seen as a key performance indicator within business and is part of the four perspectives of a Balanced Scorecard.

In a competitive marketplace where businesses compete for customers, _____ is seen as a key differentiator and increasingly has become a key element of business strategy.

a. Psychological pricing
b. Supplier diversity
c. Customer base
d. Customer satisfaction

16. _____ is either an activity of a living being (such as a human), consisting of receiving knowledge of the outside world through the senses, or the recording of data using scientific instruments. The term may also refer to any datum collected during this activity.

The scientific method requires _____s of nature to formulate and test hypotheses.

a. ADTECH
b. AMAX
c. ACNielsen
d. Observation

17. _____ in economics and business is the result of an exchange and from that trade we assign a numerical monetary value to a good, service or asset. If I trade 4 apples for an orange, the _____ of an orange is 4 - apples. Inversely, the _____ of an apple is 1/4 oranges.

a. Discounts and allowances
b. Contribution margin-based pricing
c. Price
d. Pricing

18. _____ is systematic determination of merit, worth, and significance of something or someone using criteria against a set of standards. _____ often is used to characterize and appraise subjects of interest in a wide range of human enterprises, including the arts, criminal justice, foundations and non-profit organizations, government, health care, and other human services.

Depending on the topic of interest, there are professional groups which look to the quality and rigor of the _____ process.

a. ADTECH
b. ACNielsen
c. AMAX
d. Evaluation

19. _____ or brand stretching is a marketing strategy in which a firm marketing a product with a well-developed image uses the same brand name in a different product category. Organizations use this strategy to increase and leverage brand equity (definition: the net worth and long-term sustainability just from the renowned name.) An example of a _____ is Jello-gelatin creating Jello pudding pops.

a. Web 2.0
b. Brand awareness
c. Brand extension
d. Brand orientation

20. _____ is a technique employed by forensic scientists to assist in the identification of individuals on the basis of their respective DNA profiles.

Although 99.9% of human DNA sequences are the same in every person, enough of the DNA is different to distinguish one individual from another. _____ uses repetitive sequences that vary a lot, called variable number tandem repeats

a. 180SearchAssistant
b. Power III
c. F-statistics
d. DNA profiling

Chapter 25. Contemporary Applications   113

21. A _____ is a research instrument consisting of a series of questions and other prompts for the purpose of gathering information from respondents. Although they are often designed for statistical analysis of the responses, this is not always the case. The _____ was invented by Sir Francis Galton.

a. Market research
b. Mystery shopping
c. Mystery shoppers
d. Questionnaire

22. _____ is a business management strategy aimed at embedding awareness of quality in all organizational processes. _____ has been widely used in manufacturing, education, call centers, government, and service industries, as well as NASA space and science programs.

When used together as a phrase, the three words in this expression have the following meanings:

- Total: Involving the entire organization, supply chain, and/or product life cycle
- Quality: With its usual definitions, with all its complexities
- Management: The system of managing with steps like Plan, Organize, Control, Lead, Staff, provisioning and organizing.

As defined by the International Organization for Standardization (ISO):

> '_____ is a management approach for an organization, centered on quality, based on the participation of all its members and aiming at long-term success through customer satisfaction, and benefits to all members of the organization and to society.' ISO 8402:1994

One major aim is to reduce variation from every process so that greater consistency of effort is obtained. (Royse, D., Thyer, B., Padgett D., ' Logan T., 2006)

In Japan, _____ comprises four process steps, namely:

1. Kaizen - Focuses on 'Continuous Process Improvement', to make processes visible, repeatable and measurable.
2. Atarimae Hinshitsu - The idea that 'things will work as they are supposed to' .
3. Kansei - Examining the way the user applies the product leads to improvement in the product itself.
4. Miryokuteki Hinshitsu - The idea that 'things should have an aesthetic quality' (for example, a pen will write in a way that is pleasing to the writer.)

_____ requires that the company maintain this quality standard in all aspects of its business. This requires ensuring that things are done right the first time and that defects and waste are eliminated from operations.

a. 180SearchAssistant
b. Total quality management
c. Power III
d. 6-3-5 Brainwriting

23. _____ is an advertisement in which a particular product specifically mentions a competitor by name for the express purpose of showing why the competitor is inferior to the product naming it.

This should not be confused with parody advertisements, where a fictional product is being advertised for the purpose of poking fun at the particular advertisement, nor should it be confused with the use of a coined brand name for the purpose of comparing the product without actually naming an actual competitor. ('Wikipedia tastes better and is less filling than the Encyclopedia Galactica.')

In the 1980s, during what has been referred to as the cola wars, soft-drink manufacturer Pepsi ran a series of advertisements where people, caught on hidden camera, in a blind taste test, chose Pepsi over rival Coca-Cola.

    a. GL-70   b. Comparative advertising
    c. Cost per conversion   d. Heavy-up

24. _____ refer to a collection of facts usually collected as the result of experience, observation or experiment or a set of premises. This may consist of numbers, words particularly as measurements or observations of a set of variables. _____ are often viewed as a lowest level of abstraction from which information and knowledge are derived.
    a. Mean   b. Sample size
    c. Pearson product-moment correlation coefficient   d. Data

25. _____ is a process of gathering, modeling, and transforming data with the goal of highlighting useful information, suggesting conclusions, and supporting decision making. _____ has multiple facets and approaches, encompassing diverse techniques under a variety of names, in different business, science, and social science domains.

Data mining is a particular _____ technique that focuses on modeling and knowledge discovery for predictive rather than purely descriptive purposes.

    a. Data analysis   b. Power III
    c. 6-3-5 Brainwriting   d. 180SearchAssistant

26. _____ is the process of comparing the cost, cycle time, productivity, or quality of a specific process or method to another that is widely considered to be an industry standard or best practice. The result is often a business case for making changes in order to make improvements. The term _____ was first used by cobblers to measure ones feet for shoes.
    a. Switching cost   b. Benchmarking
    c. Business strategy   d. Strategic group

27. _____ is a 'method to transform user demands into design quality, to deploy the functions forming quality, and to deploy methods for achieving the design quality into subsystems and component parts, and ultimately to specific elements of the manufacturing process.' , as described by Dr. Yoji Akao, who originally developed _____ in Japan in 1966, when the author combined his work in quality assurance and quality control points with function deployment used in Value Engineering.

_____ is designed to help planners focus on characteristics of a new or existing product or service from the viewpoints of market segments, company, or technology-development needs. The technique yields graphs and matrices.

Chapter 25. Contemporary Applications

a. Futurist
c. Power III

b. Quality function deployment
d. 180SearchAssistant

28. _____ , according to Cornish, 'the process of acquiring and analyzing information in order to understand the market (both existing and potential customers); to determine the current and future needs and preferences, attitudes and behavior of the market; and to assess changes in the business environment that may affect the size and nature of the market in the future.' ('Product', 1997, p147.)

This figure shows how the interaction between variables from producers, communication channels, and consumers vary the effectiveness of _____ which affects the performance of the sales of a new product. The product is central in a circle because it helps to direct what information is gathered and how.

a. Brand parity
c. Line extension

b. Co-branding
d. Market intelligence

29. Consumer market research is a form of applied sociology that concentrates on understanding the behaviours, whims and preferences, of consumers in a market-based economy, and aims to understand the effects and comparative success of marketing campaigns. The field of consumer _____ as a statistical science was pioneered by Arthur Nielsen with the founding of the ACNielsen Company in 1923 .

Thus _____ is the systematic and objective identification, collection, analysis, and dissemination of information for the purpose of assisting management in decision making related to the identification and solution of problems and opportunities in marketing.

a. Marketing research process
c. Logit analysis

b. Marketing research
d. Focus group

30. _____ is a broad label that refers to any individuals or households that use goods and services generated within the economy. The concept of a _____ is used in different contexts, so that the usage and significance of the term may vary.

A _____ is a person who uses any product or service.

a. Power III
c. 6-3-5 Brainwriting

b. 180SearchAssistant
d. Consumer

Chapter 26. Emerging Applications

1. _____ is a sub-discipline and type of marketing. There are two main definitional characteristics which distinguish it from other types of marketing. The first is that it attempts to send its messages directly to consumers, without the use of intervening media.
   a. Direct Marketing Associations
   b. Power III
   c. Database marketing
   d. Direct marketing

2. In marketing, customer _____, lifetime customer value (LCV), or _____ (LTV) and a new concept of 'customer life cycle management' is the present value of the future cash flows attributed to the customer relationship. Use of customer _____ as a marketing metric tends to place greater emphasis on customer service and long-term customer satisfaction, rather than on maximizing short-term sales.

   Customer _____ has intuitive appeal as a marketing concept, because in theory it represents exactly how much each customer is worth in monetary terms, and therefore exactly how much a marketing department should be willing to spend to acquire each customer.

   a. Brand infiltration
   b. Sweepstakes
   c. Value chain
   d. Lifetime value

3. _____ is defined by the American _____ Association as the activity, set of institutions, and processes for creating, communicating, delivering, and exchanging offerings that have value for customers, clients, partners, and society at large. The term developed from the original meaning which referred literally to going to market, as in shopping, or going to a market to sell goods or services.

   _____ practice tends to be seen as a creative industry, which includes advertising, distribution and selling.

   a. Marketing myopia
   b. Customer acquisition management
   c. Marketing
   d. Product naming

4. A personal and cultural _____ is a relative ethic _____, an assumption upon which implementation can be extrapolated. A _____ system is a set of consistent _____s and measures that is soo not true. A principle _____ is a foundation upon which other _____s and measures of integrity are based.
   a. Package-on-Package
   b. Perceptual maps
   c. Supreme Court of the United States
   d. Value

5. A _____ is a structured collection of records or data that is stored in a computer system. The structure is achieved by organizing the data according to a _____ model. The model in most common use today is the relational model.
   a. 180SearchAssistant
   b. Power III
   c. 6-3-5 Brainwriting
   d. Database

6. _____ is a form of direct marketing using databases of customers or potential customers to generate personalized communications in order to promote a product or service for marketing purposes. The method of communication can be any addressable medium, as in direct marketing.

   The distinction between direct and _____ stems primarily from the attention paid to the analysis of data.

Chapter 26. Emerging Applications

a. Direct marketing
b. Direct Marketing Associations
c. Power III
d. Database marketing

7. _____ is a broad label that refers to any individuals or households that use goods and services generated within the economy. The concept of a _____ is used in different contexts, so that the usage and significance of the term may vary.

A _____ is a person who uses any product or service.

a. Consumer
b. 180SearchAssistant
c. Power III
d. 6-3-5 Brainwriting

8. _____ , according to Cornish, 'the process of acquiring and analyzing information in order to understand the market (both existing and potential customers); to determine the current and future needs and preferences, attitudes and behavior of the market; and to assess changes in the business environment that may affect the size and nature of the market in the future.' ('Product', 1997, p147.)

This figure shows how the interaction between variables from producers, communication channels, and consumers vary the effectiveness of _____ which affects the performance of the sales of a new product. The product is central in a circle because it helps to direct what information is gathered and how.

a. Line extension
b. Brand parity
c. Market intelligence
d. Co-branding

9. _____ refer to a collection of facts usually collected as the result of experience, observation or experiment or a set of premises. This may consist of numbers, words particularly as measurements or observations of a set of variables. _____ are often viewed as a lowest level of abstraction from which information and knowledge are derived.

a. Pearson product-moment correlation coefficient
b. Sample size
c. Data
d. Mean

10. _____ is a term used to describe a process of preparing and collecting data - for example as part of a process improvement or similar project.

_____ usually takes place early on in an improvement project, and is often formalised through a _____ Plan which often contains the following activity.

1. Pre collection activity - Agree goals, target data, definitions, methods
2. Collection - _____
3. Present Findings - usually involves some form of sorting analysis and/or presentation.

Chapter 26. Emerging Applications

A formal _____ process is necessary as it ensures that data gathered is both defined and accurate and that subsequent decisions based on arguments embodied in the findings are valid. The process provides both a baseline from which to measure from and in certain cases a target on what to improve. Types of _____ 1-By mail questionnaires 2-By personal interview

- Six sigma
- Sampling (statistics)

a. Power III
c. 180SearchAssistant
b. 6-3-5 Brainwriting
d. Data collection

11. _____ refers to a business or organization attempting to acquire goods or services to accomplish the goals of the enterprise. Though there are several organizations that attempt to set standards in the _____ process, processes can vary greatly between organizations. Typically the word '_____' is not used interchangeably with the word 'procurement', since procurement typically includes Expediting, Supplier Quality, and Traffic and Logistics (T'L) in addition to _____.

a. Supply network
c. Purchasing
b. Drop shipping
d. Supply chain

12. _____ is a technique employed by forensic scientists to assist in the identification of individuals on the basis of their respective DNA profiles.

Although 99.9% of human DNA sequences are the same in every person, enough of the DNA is different to distinguish one individual from another. _____ uses repetitive sequences that vary a lot, called variable number tandem repeats

a. 180SearchAssistant
c. F-statistics
b. Power III
d. DNA profiling

13. _____ refers to the additional value of a commodity over the cost of commodities used to produce it from the previous stage of production. An example is the price of gasoline at the pump over the price of the oil in it. In national accounts used in macroeconomics, it refers to the contribution of the factors of production, i.e., land, labor, and capital goods, to raising the value of a product and corresponds to the incomes received by the owners of these factors. The factors of production provide 'services' which raise the unit price of a product (X) relative to the cost per unit of intermediate goods used up in the production of X. _____ is shared between the factors of production (capital, labor, also human capital), giving rise to issues of distribution.

a. Power III
c. Deregulation
b. Value added
d. Consumer spending

14. _____ is the process of extracting hidden patterns from data. As more data is gathered, with the amount of data doubling every three years, _____ is becoming an increasingly important tool to transform this data into information. It is commonly used in a wide range of profiling practices, such as marketing, surveillance, fraud detection and scientific discovery.

Chapter 26. Emerging Applications

a. Data mining
b. 180SearchAssistant
c. Structure mining
d. Power III

15. Electronic commerce, commonly known as _____ or eCommerce, consists of the buying and selling of products or services over electronic systems such as the Internet and other computer networks. The amount of trade conducted electronically has grown extraordinarily with wide-spread Internet usage. A wide variety of commerce is conducted in this way, spurring and drawing on innovations in electronic funds transfer, supply chain management, Internet marketing, online transaction processing, electronic data interchange (EDI), inventory management systems, and automated data collection systems.
   a. ACNielsen
   b. ADTECH
   c. E-commerce
   d. AMAX

16. _____ is the examining of goods or services from retailers with the intent to purchase at that time. _____ is an activity of selection and/or purchase. In some contexts it is considered a leisure activity as well as an economic one.
   a. Hawkers
   b. Discount store
   c. Shopping
   d. Khodebshchik

17. A _____ is a statement or claim that a particular event will occur in the future in more certain terms than a forecast. The etymology of this word is Latin . In regards to predicting the future Howard H. Stevenson Says, ' _____ is at least two things: Important and hard.' Important, because we have to act, and hard because we have to realize the future we want, and what is the best way to get there.
   a. 180SearchAssistant
   b. Power III
   c. Prediction
   d. 6-3-5 Brainwriting

18. _____ is a form of marketing developed from direct response marketing campaigns conducted in the 1970's and 1980's which emphasizes customer retention and satisfaction, rather than a dominant focus on 'point of sale' transactions.

_____ differs from other forms of marketing in that it recognizes the long term value to the firm of keeping customers, as opposed to direct or 'Intrusion' marketing, which focuses upon acquisition of new clients by targeting majority demographics based upon prospective client lists.

_____ refers to long-term and mutually beneficial arrangement wherein both buyer and seller focus on value enhancement through the certain of more satisfying exchange.This approach attempts to transcend the simple purchase exchange process with customer to make more meaningful and richer contact by providing a more holistic, personalized purchase, and use orn consumption experience to create stronger ties.

   a. Guerrilla Marketing
   b. Diversity marketing
   c. Global marketing
   d. Relationship marketing

19. _____ is the process of gathering and analysing information regarding customers; their details and their activities, in order to build deeper and more effective customer relationships and improve strategic decision making.

Consumer Intelligence is also the name of a leading company within the UK Research industry that is referenced in large number of Advertising campaigns by companies such as Asda, Budget Compare The Market, Churchill, Direct Line, MoneySupermarket, Norwich Union and many others.

_____ is a key component of effective Customer Relationship Management, and when effectively implemented it is a rich source of insight into the behaviour and experience of a company's customer base.

a. Customer intelligence
b. Project Portfolio Management
c. Power III
d. Pop-up ads

20. _____, a business term, is a measure of how products and services supplied by a company meet or surpass customer expectation. It is seen as a key performance indicator within business and is part of the four perspectives of a Balanced Scorecard.

In a competitive marketplace where businesses compete for customers, _____ is seen as a key differentiator and increasingly has become a key element of business strategy.

a. Psychological pricing
b. Customer base
c. Supplier diversity
d. Customer satisfaction

21. _____ is one of the four elements of marketing mix. An organization or set of organizations (go-betweens) involved in the process of making a product or service available for use or consumption by a consumer or business user.

The other three parts of the marketing mix are product, pricing, and promotion.

a. Comparison-Shopping agent
b. Distribution
c. Better Living Through Chemistry
d. Japan Advertising Photographers' Association

22.

The net present value (NPV) of all of a company's customers in terms of customer loyalty and indirectly, the revenue that the company can obtain from them.

In deciding the value of a company, it is important to know of how much value its customer base is in terms of future revenues. The greater the _____, the more future revenue in the lifetime of its clients; this means that a company with a higher _____ can get more money from its customers on average than another company that is identical in all other characteristics.

a. Marginal revenue
b. Customer equity
c. Product proliferation
d. Total cost

23. In mathematics, an _____, or central tendency of a data set refers to a measure of the 'middle' or 'expected' value of the data set. There are many different descriptive statistics that can be chosen as a measurement of the central tendency of the data items.

An _____ is a single value that is meant to typify a list of values.

Chapter 26. Emerging Applications

a. ADTECH
b. ACNielsen
c. AMAX
d. Average

24. In economics, _____ is equal to total cost divided by the number of goods produced (the output quantity, Q.) It is also equal to the sum of average variable costs (total variable costs divided by Q) plus average fixed costs (total fixed costs divided by Q.) _____s may be dependent on the time period considered (increasing production may be expensive or impossible in the short term, for example.)
 a. ACNielsen
 b. ADTECH
 c. Average cost
 d. Average variable cost

25. In economics, business, retail, and accounting, a _____ is the value of money that has been used up to produce something, and hence is not available for use anymore. In economics, a _____ is an alternative that is given up as a result of a decision. In business, the _____ may be one of acquisition, in which case the amount of money expended to acquire it is counted as _____.
 a. Variable cost
 b. Cost
 c. Fixed costs
 d. Transaction cost

26. The _____ is an expected return that the provider of capital plans to earn on their investment.

Capital (money) used for funding a business should earn returns for the capital providers who risk their capital. For an investment to be worthwhile, the expected return on capital must be greater than the _____.

 a. 180SearchAssistant
 b. 6-3-5 Brainwriting
 c. Power III
 d. Cost of capital

27. _____ is the process of estimation in unknown situations. Prediction is a similar, but more general term. Both can refer to estimation of time series, cross-sectional or longitudinal data.
 a. 6-3-5 Brainwriting
 b. 180SearchAssistant
 c. Power III
 d. Forecasting

28. A _____ attribute is one that exists in a range of magnitudes, and can therefore be measured. Measurements of any particular _____ property are expressed as a specific quantity, referred to as a unit, multiplied by a number. Examples of physical quantities are distance, mass, and time.
 a. BeyondROI
 b. Dolly Dimples
 c. Quantitative
 d. Lifestyle city

29. _____ is a field of inquiry that crosscuts disciplines and subject matters . _____ers aim to gather an in-depth understanding of human behavior and the reasons that govern such behavior. The discipline investigates the why and how of decision making, not just what, where, when.
 a. 180SearchAssistant
 b. 6-3-5 Brainwriting
 c. Power III
 d. Qualitative research

30. In statistics, _____ is a technique that can be applied to time series data, either to produce smoothed data for presentation, or to make forecasts. The time series data themselves are a sequence of observations. The observed phenomenon may be an essentially random process, or it may be an orderly, but noisy, process.

a. ACNielsen
b. ADTECH
c. AMAX
d. Exponential smoothing

31. In economics, _____s are key economic variables that economists used to predict a new phase of the business cycle. A _____ is one that changes before the economy does; a lagging indicator is one that changes after the economy has changed. Examples of _____s include stock prices, which often improve or worsen before a similar change in the economy.
    a. Perfect competition
    b. Money
    c. Recession
    d. Leading indicator

32. In statistics, a _____ rolling mean or running average, is a type of finite impulse response filter used to analyze a set of data points by creating a series of averages of different subsets of the full data set. A _____ is not a single number, but it is a set of numbers, each of which is the average of the corresponding subset of a larger set of data points. A _____ may also use unequal weights for each data value in the subset to emphasize particular values in the subset.
    a. Statistics
    b. Confounding variables
    c. Moving average
    d. Frequency distribution

33. In statistics and image processing, to smooth a data set is to create an approximating function that attempts to capture important patterns in the data, while leaving out noise or other fine-scale structures/rapid phenomena. Many different algorithms are used in _____. One of the most common algorithms is the 'moving average', often used to try to capture important trends in repeated statistical surveys.
    a. Power III
    b. 6-3-5 Brainwriting
    c. 180SearchAssistant
    d. Smoothing

34. The process of _____ involves emphasising some aspects of a phenomenon, or of a set of data -- giving them 'more weight' in the final effect or result. It is analogous to the practice of adding extra weight to one side of a pair of scales to favour a buyer or seller.

    While _____ may be applied to a set of data, for example epidemiological data, it is more commonly applied to measurements of light, heat, sound, gamma radiation, in fact any stimulus that is spread over a spectrum of frequencies.

    a. 180SearchAssistant
    b. Power III
    c. 6-3-5 Brainwriting
    d. Weighting

35. A _____ is any statistical hypothesis test in which the test statistic has a chi-square distribution when the null hypothesis is true, or any in which the probability distribution of the test statistic (assuming the null hypothesis is true) can be made to approximate a chi-square distribution as closely as desired by making the sample size large enough.

Chapter 26. Emerging Applications

Some examples of chi-squared tests where the chi-square distribution is only approximately valid:

- Pearson's _____, also known as the chi-square goodness-of-fit test or _____ for independence. When mentioned without any modifiers or without other precluding context, this test is usually understood.
- Yates' _____, also known as Yates' correction for continuity.
- Mantel-Haenszel _____.
- Linear-by-linear association _____.
- The portmanteau test in time-series analysis, testing for the presence of autocorrelation
- Likelihood-ratio tests in general statistical modelling, for testing whether there is evidence of the need to move from a simple model to a more complicated one (where the simple model is nested within the complicated one.)

One case where the distribution of the test statistic is an exact chi-square distribution is the test that the variance of a normally-distributed population has a given value based on a sample variance. Such a test is uncommon in practice because values of variances to test against are seldom known exactly.

If a sample of size n is taken from a population having a normal distribution, then there is a well-known result which allows a test to be made of whether the variance of the population has a pre-determined value.

a. Confounding variables
b. Chi-square test
c. Randomization
d. Type I error

36. _____ is a computer program used for statistical analysis.

_____ (originally, Statistical Package for the Social Sciences) was released in its first version in 1968 after being founded by Norman Nie and C. Hadlai Hull. Nie was then a political science postgraduate at Stanford University,and now Research Professor in the Department of Political Science at Stanford and Professor Emeritus of Political Science at the University of Chicago.

a. Power III
b. 6-3-5 Brainwriting
c. 180SearchAssistant
d. SPSS

37. In statistics, _____ is a collection of statistical models, and their associated procedures, in which the observed variance is partitioned into components due to different explanatory variables. The initial techniques of the _____ were developed by the statistician and geneticist R. A. Fisher in the 1920s and 1930s, and is sometimes known as Fisher's ANOVA or Fisher's _____, due to the use of Fisher's F-distribution as part of the test of statistical significance.

There are three conceptual classes of such models:

1. Fixed-effects models assumes that the data came from normal populations which may differ only in their means. (Model 1)
2. Random effects models assume that the data describe a hierarchy of different populations whose differences are constrained by the hierarchy. (Model 2)
3. Mixed-effect models describe situations where both fixed and random effects are present. (Model 3)

In practice, there are several types of ANOVA depending on the number of treatments and the way they are applied to the subjects in the experiment:

- One-way ANOVA is used to test for differences among two or more independent groups. Typically, however, the One-way ANOVA is used to test for differences among at least three groups, since the two-group case can be covered by a T-test (Gossett, 1908.)

a. Arithmetic mean
b. Interval estimation
c. ACNielsen
d. Analysis of variance

38. In statistics, _____ is used for two things;

- to construct a simple formula that will predict what value will occur for a quantity of interest when other related variables take given values.
- to allow a test to be made of whether a given variable does have an effect on a quantity of interest in situations where there may be many related variables.

In both cases, several sets of outcomes are available for the quantity of interest together with the related variables.

_____ is a form of regression analysis in which the relationship between one or more independent variables and another variable, called the dependent variable, is modelled by a least squares function, called a _____ equation. This function is a linear combination of one or more model parameters, called regression coefficients. A _____ equation with one independent variable represents a straight line when the predicted value (i.e. the dependant variable from the regression equation) is plotted against the independent variable: this is called a simple _____.

a. Linear regression
b. Descriptive statistics
c. Heteroskedastic
d. Sample size

39. In probability theory and statistics, the _____ of a random variable, probability distribution, or sample is a measure of statistical dispersion, averaging the squared distance of its possible values from the expected value (mean.) Whereas the mean is a way to describe the location of a distribution, the _____ is a way to capture its scale or degree of being spread out. The unit of _____ is the square of the unit of the original variable.

Chapter 26. Emerging Applications

a. Sample size
b. Standard deviation
c. Correlation
d. Variance

40. _____ is a statistical method used to describe variability among observed variables in terms of fewer unobserved variables called factors. The observed variables are modeled as linear combinations of the factors, plus 'error' terms. The information gained about the interdependencies can be used later to reduce the set of variables in a dataset.
   a. Likert scale
   b. Semantic differential
   c. Factor analysis
   d. Power III

41. In algebra, the _____ of a polynomial with real or complex coefficients is a certain expression in the coefficients of the polynomial which is equal to zero if and only if the polynomial has a multiple root (i.e. a root with multiplicity greater than one) in the complex numbers. For example, the _____ of the quadratic polynomial

$$ax^2 + bx + c \text{ is } b^2 - 4ac.$$

The _____ of the cubic polynomial

$$ax^3 + bx^2 + cx + d \text{ is } b^2c^2 - 4ac^3 - 4b^3d - 27a^2d^2 + 18abcd.$$

   a. Discriminant
   b. Consumption Map
   c. Lifestyle center
   d. Flighting

42. Linear _____ and the related Fisher's linear discriminant are methods used in statistics and machine learning to find the linear combination of features which best separate two or more classes of objects or events. The resulting combination may be used as a linear classifier, or, more commonly, for dimensionality reduction before later classification.

LDiscriminant analysis is closely related to ANOVA (analysis of variance) and regression analysis, which also attempt to express one dependent variable as a linear combination of other features or measurements.

   a. Geodemographic segmentation
   b. Multiple discriminant analysis
   c. Linear discriminant analysis
   d. Discriminant analysis

43. In mathematics, the _____ or Euclidean metric is the 'ordinary' distance between two points that one would measure with a ruler, which can be proven by repeated application of the Pythagorean theorem. By using this formula as distance, Euclidean space becomes a metric space (even a Hilbert space.) The associated norm is called the Euclidean norm.
   a. Euclidean distance
   b. AMAX
   c. ACNielsen
   d. ADTECH

44. _____ is a set of related statistical techniques often used in information visualization for exploring similarities or dissimilarities in data. MDS is a special case of ordination. An MDS algorithm starts with a matrix of item-item similarities, then assigns a location to each item in N-dimensional space, where N is specified a priori.
   a. Multidimensional scaling
   b. Cocooning
   c. Convenience
   d. Situational theory of publics

Chapter 26. Emerging Applications

45. _____ is a form of communication that typically attempts to persuade potential customers to purchase or to consume more of a particular brand of product or service. 'While now central to the contemporary global economy and the reproduction of global production networks, it is only quite recently that _____ has been more than a marginal influence on patterns of sales and production. The formation of modern _____ was intimately bound up with the emergence of new forms of monopoly capitalism around the end of the 19th and beginning of the 20th century as one element in corporate strategies to create, organize and where possible control markets, especially for mass produced consumer goods.
   a. ACNielsen
   b. AMAX
   c. ADTECH
   d. Advertising

46. The _____ of a statistical sample is the number of observations that constitute it. It is typically denoted n, a positive integer (natural number.)

Typically, all else being equal, a larger _____ leads to increased precision in estimates of various properties of the population.

   a. Heteroskedastic
   b. Frequency distribution
   c. Data
   d. Sample size

47. _____ is anything that is intended to save time, energy or frustration. A _____ store at a petrol station, for example, sells items that have nothing to do with gasoline/petrol, but it saves the consumer from having to go to a grocery store. '_____' is a very relative term and its meaning tends to change over time.
   a. Demographic profile
   b. MaxDiff
   c. Marketing buzz
   d. Convenience

48. _____ is a type of nonprobability sampling which involves the sample being drawn from that part of the population which is close to hand. That is, a sample population selected because it is readily available and convenient. The researcher using such a sample cannot scientifically make generalizations about the total population from this sample because it would not be representative enough.
   a. ADTECH
   b. AMAX
   c. ACNielsen
   d. Accidental sampling

49. _____ is that part of statistical practice concerned with the selection of individual observations intended to yield some knowledge about a population of concern, especially for the purposes of statistical inference. Each observation measures one or more properties (weight, location, etc.) of an observable entity enumerated to distinguish objects or individuals.
   a. Richard Buckminster 'Bucky' Fuller
   b. Sports Marketing Group
   c. AStore
   d. Sampling

50. A _____ is a type of wholesale merchant business that buys goods and bulk products from importers, other wholesalers and then sells to retailers. _____s can deal in any commodity destined for the retail market. Typical categories are food, lumber, hardware, fuel, and textiles.
   a. Jobbing house
   b. Tacit collusion
   c. Chief privacy officer
   d. Refusal to deal

51. The _____ of American Manufacturers is a multi-volume directory of industrial product information covering 650,000 distributors, manufacturers and service companies within 67,000-plus industrial categories. It was first published in 1898 by Harvey Mark Thomas as Hardware and Kindred Trades. The company stopped publishing its print products in 2006 due to declining circulation as Internet searches eroded the products' usability.

a. Futura plus
b. Free box
c. Stock management
d. Thomas Register

Chapter 1
1. c 2. a 3. d 4. d 5. b 6. c 7. d 8. d 9. d 10. a
11. d 12. a 13. d 14. d 15. d 16. d 17. d 18. d 19. a 20. d
21. d 22. d 23. b 24. b

Chapter 2
1. d 2. d 3. d 4. a 5. a 6. c 7. c 8. a 9. d 10. b
11. b 12. d 13. b 14. a 15. a

Chapter 3
1. d 2. a 3. a 4. d 5. a 6. d 7. d

Chapter 4
1. c 2. c 3. a 4. d 5. b 6. d 7. b 8. d 9. d 10. d
11. d 12. a 13. d 14. d 15. d 16. c 17. d 18. d 19. a 20. d
21. b 22. a 23. b 24. d 25. d 26. d 27. c 28. a 29. b 30. d
31. a 32. b

Chapter 5
1. d 2. a 3. d 4. d 5. d 6. d 7. d 8. b 9. d 10. b
11. d 12. a 13. b 14. d 15. d 16. a 17. d 18. c 19. d 20. d
21. d 22. d 23. d 24. c 25. d 26. d 27. d 28. a 29. d 30. b
31. a 32. d 33. c

Chapter 6
1. d 2. c 3. a 4. d 5. d 6. a 7. b 8. c 9. c 10. d
11. d 12. d 13. a 14. d 15. c 16. a 17. d 18. d 19. d 20. b
21. d 22. c 23. b 24. b 25. d

Chapter 7
1. b 2. d 3. d 4. b 5. b 6. c 7. d 8. a 9. d 10. d
11. d 12. d 13. b 14. a 15. b 16. a 17. b 18. a 19. c 20. b
21. c 22. d 23. d 24. d

Chapter 8
1. b 2. d 3. a 4. d 5. d 6. a 7. c 8. c 9. a 10. d
11. d 12. a 13. d 14. d 15. d 16. d 17. a 18. b

Chapter 9
1. b 2. d 3. a 4. d 5. b 6. a 7. a 8. d 9. a 10. a
11. d 12. d 13. c 14. d 15. d 16. d 17. d 18. d 19. d

Chapter 10
1. d 2. a 3. b 4. d 5. b 6. c 7. d 8. c

ANSWER KEY

Chapter 11
1. b   2. d   3. c   4. c   5. d   6. d   7. a   8. d   9. a   10. b
11. a   12. b   13. d   14. a   15. d   16. d   17. d   18. b   19. d   20. d

Chapter 12
1. d   2. d   3. d   4. a   5. d

Chapter 13
1. a   2. a   3. a   4. d   5. d   6. a   7. d   8. a   9. a   10. d
11. d   12. a   13. d   14. c   15. b   16. d   17. d   18. c   19. a   20. d
21. b   22. a   23. d   24. b   25. d   26. d   27. a   28. d   29. a   30. d
31. c   32. b

Chapter 14
1. d   2. d   3. d   4. d   5. d   6. b   7. a   8. b   9. d   10. c
11. d   12. a   13. d   14. d   15. a   16. b   17. d   18. c   19. c   20. d
21. d   22. c   23. d   24. b

Chapter 15
1. b   2. d   3. c   4. a   5. b   6. d   7. d   8. a   9. d   10. c
11. b   12. a   13. a   14. b   15. c   16. d   17. d

Chapter 16
1. d   2. c   3. d   4. d   5. a   6. d   7. d   8. d   9. c   10. d
11. d   12. d   13. a   14. b   15. b   16. d   17. c   18. d   19. d   20. c
21. d   22. b   23. c   24. b   25. b   26. a   27. d   28. d   29. d   30. d
31. c   32. b   33. d   34. d

Chapter 17
1. b   2. d   3. d   4. c   5. a   6. d   7. d   8. c   9. d   10. a
11. d   12. d   13. a   14. d

Chapter 18
1. d   2. d   3. b   4. d   5. d   6. d   7. d   8. a   9. a   10. c
11. d   12. d   13. d   14. d

Chapter 19
1. b   2. a   3. a   4. c   5. b   6. b   7. b   8. c   9. d   10. c
11. a   12. a   13. d   14. a   15. c

Chapter 20
1. a   2. d   3. d   4. d   5. d   6. d   7. d

Chapter 21
1. d   2. b   3. a   4. b   5. d   6. c   7. d   8. d   9. d   10. a
11. d

Chapter 22
1. d   2. a   3. a   4. d   5. b   6. b   7. b   8. b   9. b   10. b
11. b

Chapter 23
1. d   2. d

Chapter 24
1. b   2. d   3. d   4. b   5. d   6. d   7. a   8. d   9. d   10. d
11. c   12. d   13. a   14. d   15. d   16. d   17. a   18. c   19. b   20. c
21. a   22. a   23. b   24. b   25. c   26. b   27. b   28. d   29. d   30. a
31. c   32. d   33. d

Chapter 25
1. c   2. c   3. a   4. d   5. c   6. d   7. c   8. c   9. a   10. a
11. d   12. b   13. d   14. c   15. d   16. d   17. c   18. d   19. c   20. d
21. d   22. b   23. b   24. d   25. a   26. b   27. b   28. d   29. b   30. d

Chapter 26
1. d   2. d   3. c   4. d   5. d   6. d   7. a   8. c   9. c   10. d
11. c   12. d   13. b   14. a   15. c   16. c   17. c   18. d   19. a   20. d
21. b   22. b   23. d   24. c   25. b   26. d   27. d   28. c   29. d   30. d
31. d   32. c   33. d   34. d   35. b   36. d   37. d   38. a   39. d   40. c
41. a   42. d   43. a   44. a   45. d   46. d   47. d   48. d   49. d   50. a
51. d

www.ingramcontent.com/pod-product-compliance
Lightning Source LLC
Chambersburg PA
CBHW082045230426
43670CB00016B/2780